# FRANCISCAN IRELAND

Patrick Conlan ofm, was born in Limerick in 1940, educated by the Jesuits, and joined the Franciscans in 1958. He studied in Galway, Louvain and Rome, where he was ordained in 1958. In 1975 he transferred from Clonmel to Athlone, becoming vicar in 1981 and guardian in 1984. As Franciscan journalist and historian, the following are among his principal published works: *Saint Anthony's College, Louvain* (Dublin 1977), *A True Franciscan, Brother Pascal* (Athlone 1978), *Saint Isidore's, Rome* (Rome 1982) and *The Franciscans in Drogheda* (Drogheda 1987).

*Adare Friary, Co. Limerick: a reconstruction*

# FRANCISCAN IRELAND

PATRICK CONLAN OFM

THE LILLIPUT PRESS
1988

First published in 1988 by
THE LILLIPUT PRESS LTD
Gigginstown, Mullingar,
Co. Westmeath, Ireland

*British Library Cataloguing in Publication Data*

Conlan, Patrick
Franciscan Ireland
I. Franciscans, Ireland, to 1988
I. Title
271'.3'0415

ISBN 0 946640 29 7

Cover design and layout by Jarlath Hayes
Set 10½ on 12 Baskerville by
Redsetter Ltd of Dublin
and printed in England by
Billings and Sons Ltd of Worcester

*To my parents Essie and Bill*

# CONTENTS

# LIST OF ILLUSTRATIONS

# Preface

Paul-Marie Duval of the Institut de France wrote that Celtic literature reveals a taste for the supernatural, a poetry of dreams and of
fairy-like enchantment, and a quality of unreality which is in
complete contrast to Mediterranean classicism. The art of the Celts
breaks with the symmetry of classical models in its display of a
freedom of invention which reflects the Celt's independence of mind
and his constant revolt against conformity. The Celtic gods were
gods of nature – cosmic forces, rivers, mountains, animals . . . (c.f.
The UNESCO Courier, Dec. 1975). This Celtic insight shares quite
a lot with the basic Franciscan vision – a stress on the poetic and the
artistic rather than on the scientific and the rigorous, on the
individual rather than the group, and on the goodness of creation
rather than the inventions of men.

The early Franciscans first met the Celtic mentality in Ireland and
the two recognized in each other kindred souls. After a few years of
hesitation, the Irish saw in Franciscanism a reflection of their own
deep sentiments. This identification was further cemented during the
Gaelic resurgence of the fifteenth century and was completed with
the unification of the themes of faith and fatherland towards the close
of the following century. Franciscanism is still a religious tradition
closely identified with the Irish spirit.

This book seeks to fulfil a long-felt need for a general history of and
a reference work on Irish Franciscanism. It is mainly the story of the
Irish province of the Order of Friars Minor, with short sections on the
other branches of the Franciscan family in Ireland. Much of the
earlier material can be found in print elsewhere, but has been integ-
rated here into a continuous story. Little of the history from 1750 on
has been published previously. When individual items have been
inserted into their historical context, we can discover an orderly flow
of events. We gain a greater appreciation of our past. In judging other
generations we realize the historicity of our own actions.

I am aware of the danger of generalization, but I feel that this risk
has to be taken in presenting a first look at 750 years of continuous
Irish Franciscan history. I wish to thank the many friars who have
encouraged me in this project. This book is a product, not only of my
own work, but also of the co-operation of many people, to whom I am
very grateful.

*P.C.*
*Athlone, May 1978*    ix

# Preface to Revised Edition

When this book was first published it seemed likely that a more comprehensive work on the history of the Franciscans in Ireland would appear. In the event the first edition of *Franciscan Ireland* became, and is likely to remain, the standard reference work on the Irish followers of St Francis of Assisi. I have been both amazed and gratified at the manner in which my publication has been received. The first edition has been out of print since 1984. Continuing demand has prompted this second edition.

The opportunity has been taken in this new edition to reorganize the chapters into four cycles. Each begins with a major innovation (arrival, Observant reform, major restructuring, imposed renewal) leading to growth, then stasis, followed by a period of decline. It is significant that the friars are again beginning to revitalize the Order in Ireland. While little fresh material has appeared on the mediaeval period, a lot of research has been done on the nineteenth and twentieth centuries. This has been incorporated into the text. The section dealing with mediaeval architecture has been changed and expanded to include all periods. The gazetteer of friaries has been updated and individual references to the sites have been included. The main bibliography has been expanded. Finally, a list of Irish Franciscan provincials, based on that published by Fr Canice Mooney ofm, has been added.

The aim of this book remains that of being a handy reference work rather than a detailed history. I hope that it continues to serve this purpose.

*P.C.*
*Athlone, September 1988*

The publisher would like to thank Mr Vincent Hurley for his assiduous editing in the preparation of this work, and Mr Kevin O'Brien for his illustrations.

# FRANCISCAN IRELAND

# Prologue

# THE FRANCISCAN MOVEMENT

Giovanni di Pietro di Bernardone was born in 1181-2, while his father, Pietro, was on a business trip buying cloth. He was renamed Francesco, or Francis, when his father returned to Assisi. The son of wealthy parents, Francis grew up with too much money to spend, and known as a great singer and companion for a night on the town, not particularly worried about life despite his good education. As he approached his late teens, Assisi was suddenly thrown into turmoil. The citizens revolted and seized the castle which dominated the town. A civil war began and some of the nobles fled to Perugia. War then broke out between Perugia and Assisi. Francis was captured when his city was defeated at the battle of Collestrada. A year in prison, followed by a period of ill-health, gave the young man plenty of time to think. Still seeking worldly honour, he set out in 1205 to fight for the Pope against the German Emperor. But he only got as far as Spoleto, where the Lord appeared to him in a vision.

Back in Assisi Francis wandered about like a lost soul, very often praying in the partially ruined chapel of San Damiano. Towards the end of the year the figure of Christ on the Cross came to life and said to Francis: 'Go and rebuild my house, for it is falling down.' Francis continued to live as a hermit and was disowned by his father. In the summer of 1206 he took the words he had heard from the Cross literally. Francis began to physically rebuild three small chapels: San Damiano, San Pietro and the Portiuncula. Then on the feast of St Matthias, 24 February 1208, Francis heard the gospel of the Mass and thought that it had a special meaning for him: Christ ordering his disciples not to possess gold or silver, but to go and preach the kingdom of God. Francis now realized the true meaning of the vision on the Cross. He stopped building and began to go around the neighbouring villages preaching.

Almost against his wishes, the preacher began to attract companions, initially Bernard of Quintavalle, a merchant, Peter Catanii, a canon of the cathedral and a lawyer, and Giles, a young man. The first two came on 16 April 1208, regarded as the foundation day of the Franciscan Order. Francis and his companions went on various preaching trips but returned to the Portiuncula chapel below Assisi for the winter of 1208-9. By the spring of 1209 there were twelve companions and Francis brought them to Rome to receive verbal approval for their rule of life from Pope Innocent III. During 1209-10     3 lay people asked him to suggest an ideal way of life which they could practise while still in the world – the origin of the Third Order. Finally, on Palm Sunday 1212, Francis received Clare into the religious life thus giving rise to the Second Order, or the Poor Clares.

The First Order began to grow in Italy. In 1213 Francis accepted the gift of the mountain of La Verna near Florence as a place for prayer and retreat. At the general chapter of the Order held in 1217 a division into provinces was decided upon and missionaries were sent to the Orient, Germany, Hungary, France and Spain. Two years later Francis himself went to the Holy Land while sending missionaries to Morocco where they were martyred in January 1220. When Francis returned to Italy he found his Order in a state of confusion. He spent the winter of 1220-1 trying to expand the rule that had been verbally approved by Innocent III in 1209. This was presented to approximately three thousand friars who gathered for the chapter at Pentecost 1221. It was insufficient and the administrative problems were growing. St Francis withdrew to the Rieti Valley and composed his second rule which received papal approval on 29 November 1223. This is still the basic document governing the Franciscan Order. In December 1223 Francis was at Greccio, where he built the first Christmas crib. In the late summer of 1224 he was at La Verna, where he received the stigmata on 17 September. Now ill, he went on a few last preaching tours before returning to Assisi, where he died on 4 October 1226. He was canonized in Assisi on 16 July 1228 and arrangements were made to bury his body in the basilica then being built in his honour.

It is impossible to compress the message of St Francis into a few words. There seem to be three fundamental elements: a spontaneity by which he reacted instinctively to anything that seemed good and that God wanted; a conviction that an almost physical imitation of Christ was the best way to go to the Father; an ability to see the hand of God everywhere in creation, be it in a human being, an animal, or even in the very earth itself. One thing is certain: his message is as popular today as ever.

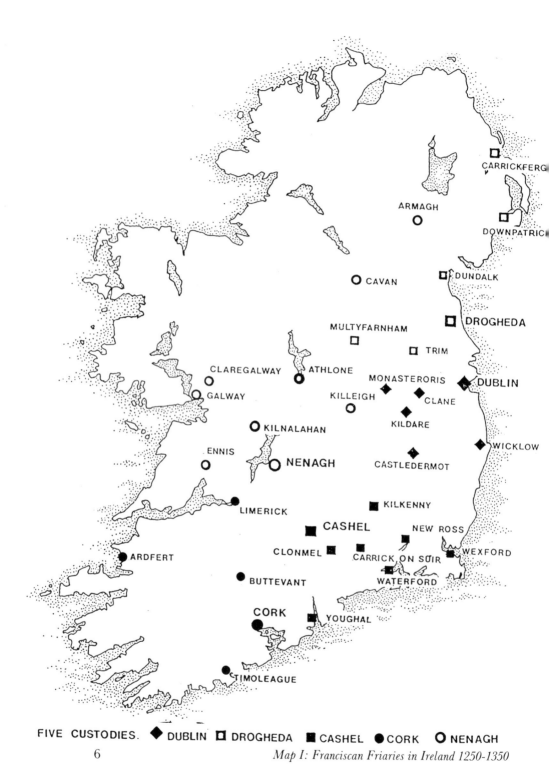

CARRICKFERG

ARMAGH ○

DOWNPATRIC

CAVAN ○

□ DUNDALK

MULTYFARNHAM □ DROGHEDA

□ TRIM

CLAREGALWAY ○ ATHLONE ○ MONASTERORIS ◆ ◆ DUBLIN

GALWAY ○ KILLEIGH ○ ◆ CLANE

KILDARE ◆

KILNALAHAN ○ ◆ WICKLOW

ENNIS ○ NENAGH ○ CASTLEDERMOT ◆

LIMERICK ● KILKENNY ■

CASHEL ■ NEW ROSS

CLONMEL ■ ■

ARDFERT ● CARRICK ON SUIR WEXFORD ■

WATERFORD ■

BUTTEVANT ●

CORK ● YOUGHAL ■

TIMOLEAGUE ●

FIVE CUSTODIES. ◆ DUBLIN □ DROGHEDA ■ CASHEL ● CORK ○ NENAGH

6                    *Map I: Franciscan Friaries in Ireland 1250-1350*

# Chapter 1

# ARRIVAL AND EXPANSION
## (*c.* 1226-1450)

Over seven hundred and sixty years ago, probably in summer of
1226, a ship arrived at the mouth of the Blackwater, just off the port
of Youghal in Co. Cork. Among the tired passengers was a group of
men dressed in worn grey habits, but whose richness of spirit
overshadowed their poverty. The harbingers of the Franciscan ideal
had arrived in Ireland.

Thus began the first cycle in the history of the followers of St
Francis of Assisi in an island which at that time was at the western
periphery of the known world. A period of rapid expansion – thirty
houses in sixty years – followed. Then the founding enthusiasm ran
out. The friars entered the mid-phase of the cycle, contented with
their achievements. There were only a handful of new foundations.
The first serious divisions between Irish and Normans within the
Order emerged. The manpower shortages after the Black Death
ushered in a period of decline. The will to move into new areas,
whether geographical, pastoral or spiritual, was missing. Only with
the Gaelic resurgence in the early fifteenth century did real sap again
begin to flow through the dry wood of Franciscanism in Ireland.

Unfortunately we know very little about these early arrivals except
from oral tradition written down long after. The friary at Youghal
has always been recognized as the first foundation of the Franciscans
in Ireland. This event must be dated between the arrival of the friars
in England in 1224 and the general chapter of the Order at Assisi in
1230. According to one tradition these friars were Romantics from
the sunny Mediterranean, coming to Ireland via northern Spain. It
seems much more likely that they were Norman-French who came
across St George's Channel from southern England. In any case, they
would have found Ireland a strange country. While the townspeople
could converse with them in the sort of bastard French spoken over
much of 'civilized' Europe, the natives spoke an unknown language
and lived according to their own distinctive laws and customs.

The well-documented history of the early Franciscans in England
gives us an idea of how the friars spread through Ireland. A group of
friars would come to a town and find a place, even a shed, to sleep, eat
and pray. Then the main group would move on, leaving behind the
nucleus of a new community. Thus, the first English friars landed at 7

Dover and formed their first community at Canterbury on 11 September 1224. The main body then moved to London, from where the friars rapidly spread to Oxford and Northampton. By 1230 sufficient friars had penetrated into Scotland for it to be erected as a full province. In 1239 Scotland was reduced to a dependent vicariate of the English province, but it remained a fairly independent unit until it vanished with the collapse of Franciscanism in England during the Reformation.

After their arrival at Youghal, it seems that the friars split into three groups. Two small groups set off to make foundations at Cork and Waterford. A larger group went to Kilkenny and thence to Dublin. From there, some went to Athlone, while others travelled up the coast to Drogheda, Downpatrick and Carrickfergus. During the next few years gaps between the early foundations were filled with houses at New Ross, Castledermot and Dundalk. Local rulers invited the friars to come to Ardfert and Claregalway. Armagh, the religious centre of Ireland, was next on the Franciscan list. Then it was the turn of the towns of Munster: Nenagh, Limerick, Cashel and Ennis. Before the end of the century there were foundations at Buttevant and Clonmel in the south; Wexford and Wicklow in the east; Trim, Kildare, Clane, Multyfarnham and Killeigh in the midlands; and Galway in the west. While the exact chronological order is subject to dispute, the friars had made a total of thirty foundations by the end of the thirteenth century.

A general chapter of the Franciscan Order was held at Assisi during Pentecost 1230. The chapter was to be the occasion for the solemn translation of the body of St Francis to the new basilica built by Br Elias. But relics were valuable in those days and the body of St Francis was hidden lest it be stolen. It remained undiscovered until 1818, when it was found in a pillar in the lower crypt of the basilica. At the chapter Fr John Parenti was elected minister general to replace Br Elias. He appointed Richard of Ingworth as the first minister provincial of the Irish Franciscan province. The concept of a province as a legal entity was not as strict then as now, and it seems certain that the friars were already in Ireland and that Richard was appointed to head an existing entity. During the lifetime of St Francis a minister provincial could be any friar in charge of a group going to a new country or district, such as Agnellus of Pisa in England. But under Br Elias the official structures were being tightened up.

Ingworth is a village about ten miles north of Norwich. Richard, an experienced administrator, was said to have been one of the first friars to preach north of the Alps. A member of the first group of friars in England, he founded the friary at Northampton. He later became custos of northern England, based at Cambridge. He acted as locum

8

for Agnellus of Pisa when the latter went to the general chapter in
1230 and the influence of Agnellus may be detected in the appointment of Richard to Ireland. Little is known of Richard's activities as
provincial in Ireland. He was involved in a rather difficult visitation
of the Scottish province in 1238, and when his period of office ended
at the general chapter of 1239 he went as a missionary to Syria, where
he died.

The next Irish provincial was a former provincial of Scotland,
John Keating, a native of Ketton in Rutland. He was appointed to
Ireland in 1239 by the new minister general, Albert of Pisa, himself
ex-provincial of England. Fr John had such a reputation for kindness
that friars from many provinces came to Ireland seeking his protection. The first known provincial chapter was held under him at Cork
in 1244. In 1251 he purchased a bible for the Irish province at Paris.
He was replaced at the general chapter at Metz in 1254.

## The Life and Work of the Early Friars

In those days one became a friar by going to the nearest friary, where
one could be admitted to the novitiate in a matter of days. Sometimes
there were problems, as when the earl of Ulster, Walter de Burgo,
sent an armed band to remove his young brother, Daniel, from the
novitiate in Dublin friary in 1258. There were no formal houses of
study for clerics. In the early years of the province only a small
number of the friars would have been priests. The young Franciscan
learned the way of life through example and practice. Later, lecturers
were assigned to those houses where there were students for the
priesthood.

Initially, a friary would have consisted of a room or building lent
by some local benefactor. The community worshipped and prayed in
a nearby chapel or parish church. All was informal with little consid-
eration given to canonical foundation documents. Then the friars
would build a dwelling suited to their requirements on a site donated
by some willing citizen. As time went on the original structure was
extended until a substantial building was constructed. Sometimes a
local ruler invited the friars to come and built a house for them
himself. In many cases the friary grounds became the burial place of
the local ruling family, for example the O'Briens in Ennis and
Limerick, the FitzMaurice family in Kildare and the O'Driscolls on
Sherkin Island. The Crown in England was also a major benefactor
to many friaries. It is often impossible to give a precise date for the
arrival of the friars in a particular area. Some sources give the date of
arrival, others the date of the initial foundation, and yet others the
date of the major benefaction. The result can sometimes be confusing.                                                                    9

**A** *Nave*
**B** *Choir*
**C** *Aisle*
**D** *Chapel*
**E** *Sacristy*
**F** *Transept*
**G** *Cloister Garth*
**H** *Tower*
**I** *West Doorway*
**M** *Residence*

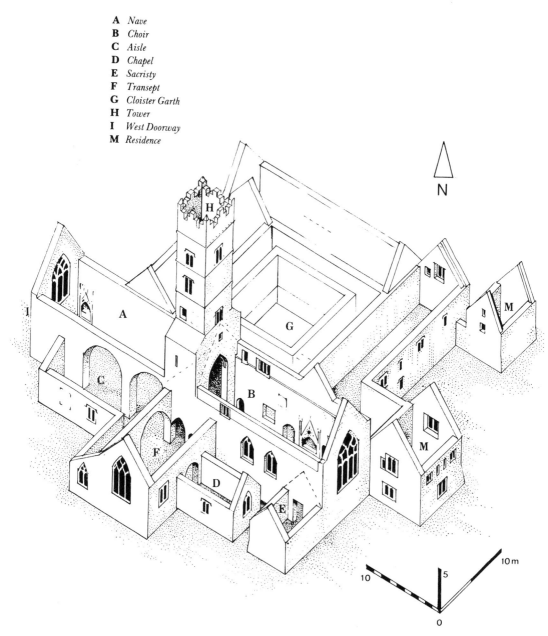

*Kilconnell Friary, Co. Galway: an isometric view*

The Ireland in which the first Franciscans arrived was in a state of transition as Norman influence began to predominate in ecclesiastical affairs. The old Irish monastic system was in decline. Its function as the centre of worship for the local community was being taken over by parish churches. This was especially true in areas under the control of the invaders, where manor and chapel went hand in hand, and in the large towns and cities where bishops with an English or continental background were in charge. Given the friars' use of parish churches elsewhere, for example in London in 1224-5, for both Mass and office, it is not surprising that in Ireland they initially worked as a leaven within existing structures rather than having their own churches. Another function of the early Irish monks had been spiritual direction. The new Orders arriving in Ireland, especially the Franciscans, took on the role of 'soul-companions' to the needy. But the initial task of the friars was to be accepted as good people. The way they lived, worked and prayed, would be the key to their success.

The main work of the friars, in addition to bearing witness to a particular style of Christian living, was preaching, using plain language with plenty of stories and images to convey their message. As early as 1240 they were preaching a Crusade and forwarding the money to Rome. It is significant that the earliest known Franciscan writing in Ireland, the *Liber Exemplorum*, is a collection of notes and stories for preachers. It was written *c.* 1270 by an English friar who was stationed in Ireland. He knew Drogheda, Cork and Dublin, and was obviously a much travelled man. One of his stories concerns fertility rites in northern Germany as related to the Dublin community by a Danish friar. Another example of a sermon is Friar Tom Quinn, preaching during a pestilence at Clonfert, who challenges the devils to come and get him, if they dare!

Some of the mediaeval clergy were widely travelled. Two friars, Simon Fitz Simeon and Hugo the Illuminator, journeyed from Ireland to the Holy Land. They went via Anglesea, London, Dover, Wissant, Paris, the Rhone, Marseilles, Bobbio, Venice and Alexandria to Jerusalem. Hugo died at Alexandria on 22 October 1324. There is also a tradition that a Friar James of Ireland accompanied Blessed Odoric of Pordenone to China in 1316-20.

There are a number of other Irish Franciscan writings of the same period in addition to the *Liber Exemplorum*. A Norman friar made a collection of French, English and Latin songs and poems in Munster *c.* 1325; the *Annals of Nenagh* and the *Annals of Friar John Clyn* of Kilkenny were written during the mid-fourteenth century. Finally there is a mysterious theological treatise on the seven deadly sins, *De Veneno*, usually attributed to a Friar Malachy of Limerick and dated *c.* 1285.

## The Problem of the Two Nations

In the early stages the Franciscans in Ireland worked mainly among the Norman townspeople. The provincials were generally of English birth, although a Gilbert of Slane (or Clane) held office c. 1226. The Franciscan charisma is all-embracing, and the friars soon began to mix with the Irish. The evidence suggests that both races lived together in the same friaries. By the end of the thirteenth century the friars were inevitably caught up in the political conflict between the two nations. Thus a Franciscan bishop of Kildare, Nicholas Cusack, reported to King Edward I:

The peace of the land is frequently disturbed by secret counsels ... which certain insolent religious of Irish tongue . . . hold with the Irish. Thus in dangerous districts Irish sympathisers should be removed from their convents and replaced by good and carefully selected English.

The report of a royal commission in 1284-5 is more explicit: 'The Dominicans and Franciscans make too much use of that [Irish] language.' It is worth noting that the Irish Franciscans formed an independent province from 1230, albeit with the English Crown having a certain right of veto over the person elected or appointed minister provincial. He was elected by the province between 1239 and 1291 and again after 1469. Otherwise he was appointed by the minister general. The Irish Dominicans, in contrast, remained a vice-province of England until as late as 1536. The Irish Carmelites became independent c. 1305, while Irish Augustinians had obtained some freedom by the end of the fourteenth century.

The tension between the Irish and the Normans towards the end of the thirteenth century gave rise to a problem of two nations in one country which lasted for nearly two hundred years. The English authorities ran a European-style church. They used their contacts with Rome to advantage, so that Irish bishops had to obtain the royal consent before they were consecrated. But the old Celtic Church remained in the Irish areas, admittedly with a Roman flavour since the reforms of the twelfth century. In practice the two nations solved their problems by keeping apart. There is little evidence of dissension at local level among the Franciscans, but there was a struggle for control of the province itself.

A provincial chapter opened in Cork on 10 June 1291 to which some of the friars came armed with Papal Bulls. A chronicler of the subsequent events remarks: 'Papal Bulls always excite men.' The issue was control of the province. Initially the Irish won by force of numbers. Then fighting broke out. The Norman townspeople came to the rescue of their fellow friars. Sixteen friars were killed. By coinci-
dence the minister general, a Frenchman named Raymond Godef-

rey, happened to arrive soon after on one of his long voyages through Europe. The result of his visit was far reaching. A decision was taken that the Irish could not be trusted to rule themselves. Within a couple of years direct rule from Rome was imposed. For the next 160 years the Irish provincial was appointed by the minister general and was always of English or Norman stock.

The problem of the two nations in Ireland underlies most of the history of the fourteenth century. One solution tried within the Irish Franciscans was the division of the province into four or five administrative units called custodies. The composition of each one was fluid. While one custody was always Irish, the others were always Norman.

Given the political conditions, it is not surprising that the civil authorities tried to restrict the entry of the Irish into religious orders under certain circumstances. A parliament at Kilkenny in 1310 ordered a complete prohibition on the reception of Irish into religious orders in the 'terre Engleis' (the area governed by the English). But soon this particular statute was revoked.

When Edward Bruce landed in Ireland in May 1315, Franciscan reaction was mixed. Within a month of his arrival, his forces had sacked Dundalk friary. Yet support for him grew among the Irish friars. On the other side, the English king, Edward II, appealed to Rome for a condemnation of his opponent. The Irish Franciscan provincial, Thomas Godman, was sent to the Pope. He was accompanied by Geoffrey of Aylsham, a politically reliable Franciscan of English blood and the royal nominee for the vacant see of Cashel. Action in Rome was slowed by the delay in the election of Pope John XXII. During the delay, Castledermot friary was burned in 1317. In reply to the king, a group of Irish chieftains sent a remonstrance, sometimes taken as the first expression of Irish nationalism, to the pope in 1318. Among other things, this document accuses a Norman friar of claiming that 'it is no sin to kill a man of Irish birth, and if he did such a thing, he would not hesitate from celebrating mass'. In the end the pope took the diplomatic way out. While condemning Bruce, John XXII rejected the nomination of Geoffrey for Cashel.

The problem of the political reliability of the Irish is seen among the Franciscans at the provincial chapter which met in Dublin in 1324. Special judges appointed by the pope found that the conduct of the friars in Cork, Limerick, Buttevant, Ardfert, Nenagh, Claregalway, Galway and Athlone was politically suspect. The chapter decreed that no Irishman could be guardian of one of these houses and all Irish friars, except for some of the most trustworthy, were to be removed from them. In practice it would seem that the rules were not applied too strictly, yet the authorities remained watchful. The royal alms for Athlone was transferred to Cashel in 1327, since the Athlone friars could no longer be trusted. Thus three years after the

13

0    10    20 cm

*St Francis, Askeaton Friary, Co. Limerick*

supposed exclusion of disloyal friars from Athlone in 1324, there were no longer sufficient loyal friars in the community! This problem of the two nations remained until the next century, and reached a high point with the Statutes of Kilkenny in 1366. It slowly faded as the two nations began to fuse more and more until it was submerged by the Gaelic resurgence after the mid-fifteenth century.

## The Irish Franciscans in the Later Middle Ages

By the later Middle Ages the friars had become well established in Ireland. Several became bishops. Friar Thomas Quinn was the first Irish Franciscan, and perhaps the very first Franciscan to be elected (not simply appointed) to an Irish bishopric. This was in the diocese of Elphin. However, he was not confirmed to the see by the king. Following another election and after a dispensation had been obtained, since he was the son of a priest, he was consecrated Bishop of Clonmacnoise in 1252. Other Irish Franciscans who became bishops included: Dr Michael Maglachlyn of Derry (1319-24), Dr Robert le Petit of Annaghdown (1325-8), Dr Thomas de Braken-bergh of Leighlin (1349-60), and Dr Bernard O'Connor of Ross, later of Limerick (1379-98). Perhaps the most famous Irish Franciscan bishop of this period was Dr Richard Ledred of Ossory, whose effigy is in St Canice's Cathedral, Kilkenny. Since he was an Englishman and a member of the English province, the king had no difficulty in confirming his appointment as bishop. Seemingly consecrated by Pope John XXII, Richard began his career with enthusiasm. He called synods, promulgated statutes, restored the cathedral, reformed the liturgy and composed upwards of sixty Latin hymns. He then came into conflict with Alice Kyteler and her son William Outlaw, accusing them of a variety of offences including heresy and witchcraft. The diocese was rent asunder in the ensuing distur-bances. Under pressure, Bishop Ledred fled to England and spent the remainder of his life as a supplicant before the popes at Avignon, where he died in 1360.

An interesting side-light on relations between the friars and the bishops is provided by the request made by Bishop Maurice of Ross in 1265 that he be allowed to relinquish his see in order to join the friars and do penance for his misdeeds and maladministration.

The creative energy of the thirteenth century died down as the friars settled into a period of consolidation. There were few new foundations, although existing houses were extended. Some local rulers invited the Franciscans to their territories. New friaries were built at Carrickbeg, Cavan, Monasteroris and Timoleague. The friars took over the only Irish Carthusian foundation at Kinalehin.

In August 1348 the Black Death arrived in Ireland, striking first in Howth and Drogheda. The Franciscan chronicler, Friar John Clyn, 15 declares that fourteen thousand people had died in Dublin by Christmas, as well as twenty-five friars in Drogheda and twenty-three in Dublin. By Lent 1349 the plague had come to Kilkenny and it seems that Clyn himself was one of its victims. In many sectors of Church life, particularly among the monastic Orders, there was a lowering of standards as superiors tried to build up sufficient numbers to provide a viable community life. There is no evidence to indicate particular problems among the Franciscans at this stage, unless one counts the seizure, by force of arms, of timber belonging to Sir Robert Preston by the guardian of Cashel in 1363! An indication that the friars were not badly affected comes from the foundation of two new houses: Kinalehin, abandoned by the Carthusians, was taken over c. 1371, and Ballabeg on the Isle of Man founded in 1367. The Irish province also evolved its own customs, such as electing superiors by the universal vote of the community.

As the Order became more clerical the friars came into conflict with the diocesan clergy over such matters as absolution in reserved cases, permission to preach, the right to quest and the right to bury people in friary ground. Thus in 1266 the friars of Armagh opened a cemetery, while in 1309-10 the bishop of Ardfert was in dispute with the friars about burial rights. Similar disputes arose between the friars of Carrickfergus and the Dominicans of Drogheda in 1317, the friars of Trim and the Dominicans of Mullingar in 1318, and the Cistercians and the friars of Dublin in 1291. Archbishop de Bicknor of Dublin limited the questing rights of the friars, among others, c. 1320. Lady chapels, often built to accommodate burials, were added to friary churches, for example Kildare in 1328, and Dublin around the same time. The rights of the friars were spelled out in the Bull *Super cathedram* of Boniface VIII in 1300. Although this was withdrawn by Benedict XI in 1304 it was re-issued by Clement V in 1311.

In Ireland matters came to a head under Richard Fitzralph, Archbishop of Armagh 1346-60. A native of Dundalk, he had grown up knowing the friars well, and may have been educated in Dundalk Friary. Some members of his family were friars and it is likely that the provincial in 1332, John Fitzralph, was a relative. He was quite friendly with the Franciscans until 1350 when he suddenly began to preach against their exemption, probably because of the extreme administrative problems which he had uncovered in his diocese. In 1356 he brought his claims to the papal court at Avignon, where he fought a losing battle. As a temporary solution, the Bull *Super cathedram* was re-issued in 1357 and the Bull *Vas electionis* of John XXII was re-issued the following year. Richard died in Avignon in 1360 and his body was brought back to Ireland for burial. A cult built up around him and as late as 1437 a penitent was ordered to go barefoot to the tomb of St Richard of Dundalk.

However, the basic disputes about rights continued. John Whitehead, a Master of Theology, supported by the archbishop of Armagh, began a preaching crusade against the friars in 1409. The matter became sufficiently famous to be cited at the University of Paris. Whitehead added a further statement to the usual accusations: 'Friars asking the privilege of hearing confessions . . . are in mortal sin and excommunicated; friars are not pastors of the true flock but madmen, thieves and wolves.'

The various orders in Ireland formed a league to defend themselves and sent an Augustinian and a Franciscan to the Pope. A condemnation of Whitehead's teachings quickly followed. One reason why such disputes took so long to settle was uncertainty as to the value of certain papal decrees, in particular those of John XXII, due to the Great Western Schism. The issue was settled by the decree *Regnans in excelsis* of Alexander V, issued in October 1409.

The old arguments broke out again in 1438. The instigator was Master Philip Norreys of Dublin, who had just returned from studying at Oxford. Norreys was first condemned by Eugene IV in *Exhibita nobis* (1440) and again by Nicholas V in *Dudum felicis* (1448). He faded into obscurity and died in 1465.

There are few extant writings by Irish Franciscans of this period. However, we have evidence of serious work in the area of study. While some rural friaries seem to have had small quasi-bardic schools for secular study, each of the larger friaries probably had its lectors in philosophy and theology. There is evidence of lectors at Ennis, Ardfert, Armagh, Askeaton, Dublin, Nenagh, Limerick, and later at Drogheda and Galway. Some Irish friars studied on the Continent. A Friar Denis of Ireland was at Paris in 1303. Philip Torrington ofm, afterwards archbishop of Cashel, studied at Oxford and Cambridge. There were two Irish friars at Strasbourg *c.* 1375. Thomas O'Colman ofm, an unsuccessful nominee for the diocese of Armagh, had studied at Paris, Oxford, Cambridge and Lincoln. In 1441 there was one Irish friar at Bologna, three at Cologne and one at Cambridge. The friars had also been involved in the effort to set up a university in Ireland in 1320.

At the beginning of the fifteenth century a spirit of weariness seemed to pervade the Church in Ireland. Worldwide administrative expediency had led the ministers general of the order to seek extensive dispensations from previous legislation so that the friars could own and administer property. Certain groups of friars, even within the one friary, were entitled to privileges. The original enthusiasm of the followers of St Francis had definitely burned out and a decline

17

had set in. In Ireland houses were enlarged. The friars had become extensive property owners, for instance Carrickbeg had 150 acres with twelve houses and ten gardens, while Castledermot had ten acres, six small houses and a water-mill. Administration went on normally, with regular mention of the minister provincial attending the general chapter. In 1405 this was held in Munich and on the way back the provincial, John, was captured by pirates and ransomed for twenty marks. The value placed on him is an indication that the infusion of energy and life brought to Ireland by the first Franciscans had run its course.

*Snipe, Waterford Friary*

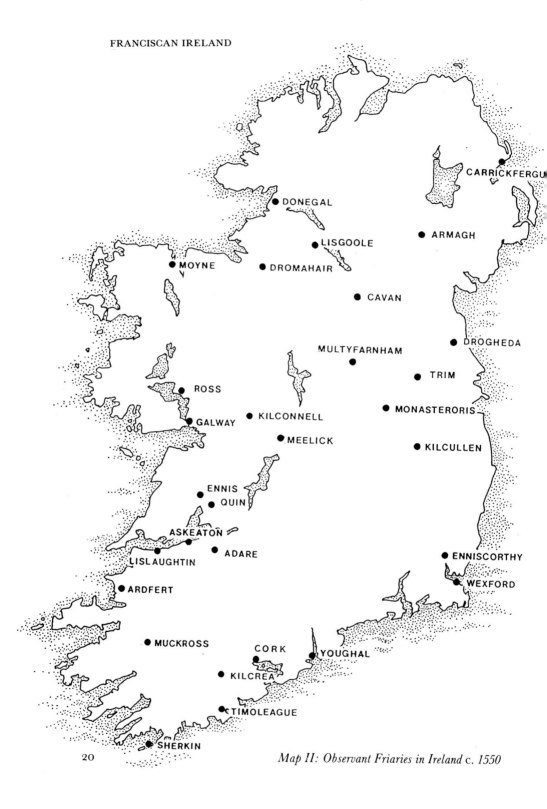

CARRICKFERGU

● DONEGAL

● ARMAGH

● LISGOOLE

● MOYNE     ● DROMAHAIR

● CAVAN

● DROGHEDA

MULTYFARNHAM

● TRIM

● ROSS

● MONASTERORIS

● GALWAY     ● KILCONNELL

●MEELICK

● KILCULLEN

ENNIS
● QUIN

ASKEATON

● ENNISCORTHY

● ADARE

LISLAUGHTIN
●WEXFORD

●ARDFERT

● MUCKROSS

CORK     ●YOUGHAL

● KILCREA

●TIMOLEAGUE

●SHERKIN

20

*Map II: Observant Friaries in Ireland c. 1550*

# Chapter 2

# OBSERVANT REFORM TO THE REFORMATION (1450-1606)

The first signs of a new spirit among the Irish Franciscans emerge towards the end of the fourteenth century. The friars began to write in Irish, for example the poems of Tadhg Camchosach (Cruikshanks) Ó Dálaig (*floruit c.* 1400) and, much later, those of Pilib Bocht Ó hUiginn (died 1487). These poets were just one sign of the Gaelic resurgence in literature, the arts, music and architecture which flourished in the fifteenth century. New friaries were built and old ones updated. The flamboyant style which then appeared marked a high-point in Irish Franciscan mediaeval architecture.

The old tradition of strict observance of the Franciscan rule re-emerged on the Continent during the fourteenth century, especially under Paul of Trinci (sixteen houses in Central Italy by 1380). The movement was taken over by the Four Pillars of the Observance who joined the Order early in the fifteenth century: Bernardine of Sienna (in 1402), John Capistran (in 1415), Albert of Sartiano (also 1415) and James of the Marches (in 1416). They sought a return to a stricter application of the ideals of St Francis. Their movement, known as the Observant Reform, was first approved by the general chapter of the Order at Assisi in 1430. The friars who did not share the spirit of the reform were known as Conventuals. Despite tensions between them, both parties remained within the same Order for nearly a century. Finally the differences became too great. On 29 May 1517 Pope Leo X created two distinct Orders with the Bull *Ite et Vos*.

## Observants and Conventuals

In Ireland, the desire to lead a stricter form of the Franciscan life and the Gaelic resurgence went hand in hand. After *c.* 1400 individual friars began to live the newer form of life in remote houses in Irish districts. Individual reformers then came together to form groups. The next step was an actual foundation. Apparently advantage was taken of a permission granted in 1433 by Pope Eugene IV to Sioda Cam MacNamara, the local Gaelic chieftain, to build a new friary on the remains of a de Clare castle at Quin in Co. Clare. This was the first actual Observant foundation. The second was at Muckross, near Killarney, founded by the McCarthy family *c.* 1445.

In law both of these new houses remained subject to the Irish 21 provincial. He was still appointed from outside and was usually of Norman descent. As such he favoured the Conventual party within the Order. Rather than have houses subject to him, the Irish Observants wished to establish communities directly under the ultramontane Observant vicar general of the Order. Permission was granted for two such houses in Co. Cork in 1449, Sherkin, and either Kilcrea or Bantry, but it would seem that these were not built until after 1460. In the interval Moyne was built some time before 1456. On completion it was immediately taken over as the first true Irish Observant friary, subject to the ultramontane vicar general.

On the Continent the Observants were involved in a change of lifestyle. While this was also true in Ireland, the movement here became part of the problem of the two nations. Generally the Observants prospered in the Irish areas and moved into the north and northwest, while the Conventuals remained within the Pale and in the cities. The shortage of manpower among the Conventuals is indicated by permission granted to them in 1469 to receive friars from other custodies into houses in the custody of Dublin. Lack of vocations seems the most likely reason why the Conventuals later made foundations in areas where the Observants had been successful.

Another important change took place at about the time the Observant Reform got under way. The law by which the minister provincial was appointed directly from Rome was altered. Fr William O'Reilly, an Irishman, was appointed provincial in 1445. He was removed from office in 1448 when the English Court objected that 'our progenitors have ordered that none of Irish blood, name and nation shall be minister . . . for the numerous mischiefs that before this (they have) caused'. We do not know the details, but Fr William seems to have been re-appointed around 1450 and continued in office until 1471. Towards the end of his term, it becomes obvious that he was elected, not appointed by Rome. This ended a situation which had lasted since the chapter at Cork in 1291.

The Irish Observants seem to have been greatly influenced by their French brethren. Communications were slow and the Observant constitutions of 1451 do not seem to have been immediately introduced into Ireland. These were the Constitutions of Barcelona and they remained in use in Ireland until well into the seventeenth century despite being superseded by the Statutes of Toledo in 1583. One Irish Observant, Fr Nehemias O'Donohue, attended the stormy general chapter at Rome in 1458. In his absence, the Irish reformers discovered their right to have an Observant vicar provincial and elected Fr Malachy O'Clune to the post. At Rome, the newly elected pope, Pius II, issued a bull reorganizing the Observants. The situation in Ireland became so confused that Pius had to issue a decree in August 1460 appointing Fr Nehemias as the Irish Observant vicar provincial. This decree marks the point at which the Irish Observants attained maturity. From 1460 until 1517 the Irish province was ruled by a Conventual minister provincial and an Observant vicar provincial. The province, like the Order, split into two in 1517.

The official recognition of the Observants in Ireland in 1460 gave a new impetus to expansion. Within a year, the reformers had taken over the old friaries at Youghal, Timoleague and Multyfarnham. They soon moved into those parts of Ireland which had never been touched by English influence, with new foundations at such sites as Sherkin, Bantry, Kilcrea, Lislaughtin, Donegal and Dromahair. The Conventuals also tried to expand into these areas, with foundations in such places as Monaghan, Galbally, Stradbally and Aran. This was also a period of great architectural vitality. In addition to new buildings, many old friaries were enlarged by the addition of chapels or renovated, with new windows and towers being inserted. The most beautiful Franciscan friaries date from this period, for example, Moyne, Lislaughtin, Kilconnell, Adare and especially Dromahair. Built in 1508 at Creevelea, beside Dromahair, Co. Leitrim, this was the last Franciscan friary to be constructed in mediaeval Ireland. It is a typical example of the flamboyant style of the period and is arguably the most beautiful of all mediaeval Franciscan sites in the country.

It was in this period that the Irish province attained its maximum size of about sixty guardianates. A reasonable guess would put the total number of friars at around six hundred.

When Pope Leo X split the Order into two Fr Philip Ó Maighreáin became the first Irish Observant provincial. The name of the corresponding Conventual provincial is not known. The two parts of the province lived in reasonable harmony. As the number of friars varied, a friary occasionally changed its loyalty from one part of the province to the other. Sometimes this was due to the influence of the local chieftain, as when the Observants of Donegal took over Carrickfergus in 1497. But there were also occasional disputes about which friary belonged to whom, such as between Galway and Armagh in 1533.

The most notable of the Irish Conventuals was the theologian Fr Maurice O'Fihely. He joined the friars c. 1475 and studied at Oxford. He first emerged into prominence in 1488 when he was regent of studies at the Franciscan College in Milan. In 1491 he obtained a similar post at Padua and became a leading member of the Scotistic school there. This interest was probably based on a mistaken belief that John Duns Scotus was an Irishman. Fr Maurice, or *Flos Mundi*  23

**B** *Choir*
**C** *Aisle*
**D** *Chapel*
**E** *Sacristy*
**F** *Transept*
**G** *Cloister Garth*
**H** *Tower*
**I** *West Doorway*
**J** *Chapter House*
**K** *Kitchen*
**L** *Dormitory*
**N** *Refectory*
**P** *Day Room*

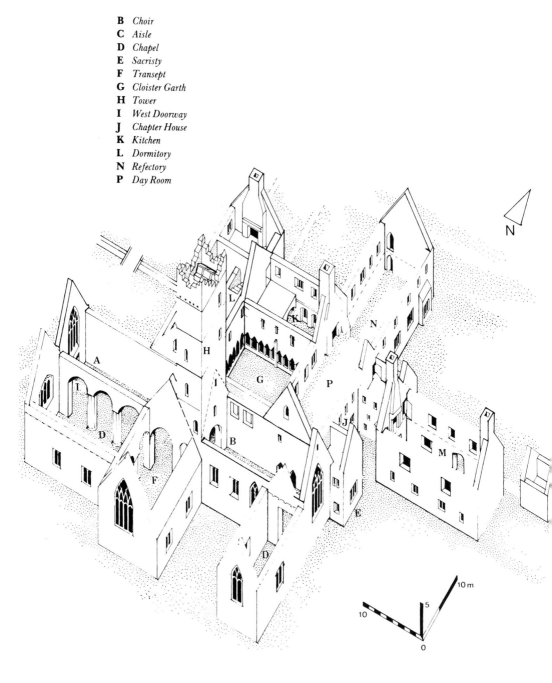

*Moyne Friary, Co. Mayo: an isometric view*

(The Flower of the World) as he was known to his contemporaries, prepared a four-volume edition of Scotus, which was printed in Venice in 1506, and published commentaries on the works of Scotus. He was an influential figure at the general chapter of the Conventuals in 1506. That same year he was appointed Archbishop of Tuam. In this capacity, he attended the fifth Lateran Council in 1512. Soon after, he began his return journey to Ireland, but died in Galway on 24 June 1513 before reaching Tuam.

## The Suppression of the Monasteries

The Reformation in Ireland is a very complex topic. In its early stages it is best considered as an extension of English law and custom to Ireland. This is also the case with the Suppression of the Irish monasteries. Abbeys had generally become very rich by this time. Communities were small. There was a flourishing trade in subletting monastic properties. The first stages of the Suppression can be seen as the nationalization of these resources by the king and their transfer to his favoured friends. In contrast to the abbeys, friaries were generally small. They were not very rich and had vigorous communities. They were only caught up in the initial suppression because the legal mind did not like an unfinished job and because many local leaders wanted to share in the spoils.

The Irish 'Act of Supremacy' and the first legislation suppressing the monasteries were introduced in the parliament of 1536. The Supremacy legislation was passed in May without any difficulty. Parliament dragged its feet over the Suppression Bill, which was not passed until October 1537. This delay had less to do with religion than with practical politics and patronage resulting from the appointment of Lord Grey as Deputy. In fact the Suppression had already begun, but only of a few large abbeys within the Pale.

The Four Masters give an account of these events from a Franciscan point of view:

Heresy and new wandering from the right path in England as a result of pride and arrogance, of avarice and evil disposition . . . . Englishmen turned against the Pope . . . and proclaimed the King in his own dominions supreme head of the Church of God . . . . they wiped out the Orders to whom worldly possessions are allowed . . . as well as the four mendicant Orders . . . they broke down the monasteries . . . sold their roofs and bells . . . they burned and broke the famous images, shrines and relics of the saints . . . they burned the celebrated image of Our Lady of Trim . . . and also the Staff of Jesus in Dublin . . . although the persecution of the Roman emperors against the Church was great, it is doubtful if Rome ever produced a persecution as great as this.

Since the Conventual houses were generally richer and were situated in areas under English control, they bore the full brunt of the    25 initial suppression of the monasteries under Henry VIII. At that time, some twenty-two friaries remained under the Conventual provincial. Many of these houses seem to have been understaffed. Most of them were in regions accessible to the commissions involved in suppressing or confiscating the monasteries, and their communities were rapidly dispersed. In exceptional circumstances, some friars were killed. Most were able to live on with help from the local people. A few joined up with the Observant friars. When the Conventual community at Monaghan was dispersed by an English army in 1540, Fr Raymond MacMahon went to live with the Observant community at Multyfarnham, where he died many years later having attained a reputation for sanctity.

With the break-up of the community life, it proved impossible to train new friars. Eventually the Irish Conventual province ceased to exist as an independent unit. From at least 1556 the Irish and Scottish provinces were governed by an appointed commissary general. Through the influence of Shane O'Neill, the Irish Conventuals did get permission to elect a provincial in 1564, but in December of that year an Italian, Jerome Fiorati, was appointed to the post. The remaining Conventuals seem to have joined the Observants as a body, probably in 1566-7. They remained near their old friaries. When the English raided Roscrea in 1579, they captured two Conventuals. Fr Tadhg O'Daly was killed when he refused to apostatize. His companion friar was released when he gave in to this request. When Fr Donagh Mooney ofm gave a mission in the area in 1611, the ex-friar repented, was readmitted to the friars and afterwards led a life of penitence for his sin.

By 1600 the Conventual Franciscans had, for all practical purposes, ceased to exist in Ireland. The reason for their downfall was twofold. Their more comfortable life made them less resilient and the location of their friaries in English-controlled areas made them easier targets for the authorities.

George Brown, an ex-Augustinian, was appointed archbishop of Dublin in 1536. Late in 1537 he started a campaign to administer the oath of Supremacy and to persuade the friars to preach royal supremacy. While many took the oath, they did not bother about its implications. A campaign of passive resistance started. Archbishop Brown then attempted to absorb the Observant friars within Conventual communities. This policy had been quite successful in England, where the Observants were small in number. It could not work in Ireland, where they were both numerous and active. Morale was high among the Irish Observants on the eve of the Suppression. Unlike the situation in England, where friars were the object of jokes, in Ireland they were well liked and respected. Thus an ambassador

26

could report in 1534 that among the wild Irish the Observants were feared, obeyed, and almost adored, not only by the peasants but by the lords. The 'poor friar beggars' were attentive to preaching the word of God in both English and Irish areas. For instance there is evidence for some sort of a country mission organized by the friars around Kilkenny in 1537. The friars in Galway were strongly defending the right to sanctuary in their church in the 1530s, and the friars of Donegal gave spiritual advice to local chieftains. In particular they persuaded the chief of the O'Gallaghers that bloodshed was unlawful with the result that he tried to take prisoners rather than cause injury. That they were learned men is shown by the inventory of Youghal friary library which, in 1494, contained a hundred books, nearly all manuscripts: including thirty volumes of Scholastic theology, twenty-four on scripture, ten on canon law, fourteen on spirituality and a dozen on sermons. The library continued to expand at the rate of a volume a year up to the next inventory in 1523.

Upset by his failure to deal with the Observants in this way, Archbishop Brown proceeded to suppress the Franciscan houses in Dublin and Kilcullen in the spring of 1539. By the autumn the campaign had spread to all parts of Ireland under English influence, and by the end of 1540 most of the friaries in the more accessible areas had been suppressed. Generally these houses yielded little to the royal funds. The buildings were handed over to new masters. The communities were dispersed. However, there was no real pressure to conform until the reign of Edward VI.

One of the first to preach publicly against the new laws was Dr Saul ofm, in Waterford on the first Sunday of Lent, 10 March 1538. As a result he was imprisoned in Dublin Castle. A report by a private agent, Thomas Agard, to Thomas Cromwell on 5 April 1538 reveals that the Observant element in all Orders, including the Franciscans, was aware of the trend of events:

So that here (in Ireland) the blood of Christ is clean blotted out of all men's hearts, what with that monster, the Observants, as they will be called most holiest, so that there remains more virtue in one of their coats and knotted girdles than ever was in Christ and His Passion.

In 1540 the vicar provincial of the Franciscan Observants rushed to Rome, warning all the authorities on his route of what was happening. At the same time the more unscrupulous of the laity began to reap the financial benefits of Suppression. This was especially true since it was the policy of the new Lord Deputy, St Leger, to 'kill Rome's rule by kindness'. Initial efforts to introduce the Counter-Reformation to the country through political means, such as the Geraldine league, failed. The Irish remained Catholic, but in the pre-

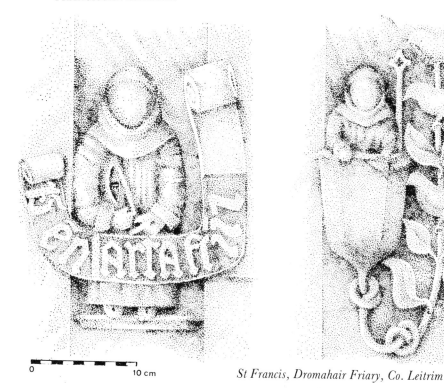

0        10 cm                    *St Francis, Dromahair Friary, Co. Leitrim*

Reformation mediaeval tradition. It took many years before Counter-Reformation Catholicism became the norm in Ireland.

The Franciscans were no exception. Well respected by the people, they were effective preachers against the new religion. Cut off from main-stream Catholicism and the effects of the Council of Trent (1545-63), they sought a return to the pre-Reformation conditions. This is the reason many clerics were ambiguous in their attitude towards the changes brought in by Henry VIII.

A classic example is the Franciscan archbishop of Cashel, Myler Magrath. He was born *c.* 1522 in Co. Donegal. His family were hereditary erenaghs of St Patrick's Purgatory on Lough Derg and thus were both important members of the nobility and also holders of high ecclesiastical office. He joined the Conventual friars probably at Downpatrick, and studied for a while on the Continent. Soon after his return to Ireland, he was sent to Rome to secure the see of Down and Connor for one of the young O'Neills. He proved such a good diplomat, that he obtained the see for himself in October 1565, yet retained the friendship of the O'Neills!

Soon after this, he judged the way the wind was blowing and he submitted to Queen Elizabeth at Drogheda on 31 May 1567. In return he received confirmation in his see, but as a Protestant prelate. He added Clogher to Down and Connor in 1570, and Cashel and Emly in the following year. He was unfortunate in that his first wife died early in marriage, but he later married Annie O'Meara. By pleading his poverty, he added the dioceses of Waterford and Lismore to his collection in 1580 and those of Killala and Achonry in 1607.

This does not mean that he was a convinced Protestant. He was extremely avaricious, proud and a consumate politician. Even his persecution of Catholics was two-edged. He arrested a number of friars for preaching against the Queen in 1571, but rapidly released them when James FitzMaurice FitzGerald threatened to burn his property. In 1582 a letter he had written from London was seized and found to contain warnings to certain Catholic bishops and priests of their imminent arrest. With his active co-operation, his wife warned many priests of intended raids.

He was declared a notorious heretic when the Holy See deprived him of the see of Down and Connor in 1580. He entered into frequent and very secret negotiations with several friars with the intention of reverting to Catholicism. The greatest secret of his life remains whether he was received back into the Catholic Church before his death in December 1622 at the reputed age of one hundred. His career shows how difficult it can be to define the religious and political affiliations of the time.

The friars hoped that the Catholic Queen Mary, who had succeeded King Edward VI, would restore the conditions which had prevailed before the Henrician Reformation. They needed houses to train novices. Two friars went to London in 1554 to request the return of Multyfarnham (where the friars were still living), Carrickfergus, Enniscorthy, Kilcullen and Trim. Much though she would like to have granted their request, political and financial conditions dictated that Mary could not do so. The friars continued to live in small communities, occasionally using their old buildings, when local rulers were sympathetic. For instance, seven of the eight friaries in Co. Galway were in operation in the 1550s, six in the original buildings, and four of these lasted nearly to the end of the century. Franciscans in other countries were willing to help, and individual friars frequently went to the Continent, where they could study and work in peace.

## Persecution under Queen Elizabeth I

Queen Elizabeth I came to the throne in 1558. Initially, nothing changed, except that a few of the larger communities had to disperse. Trouble arose following the formation of the Desmond confederation    29 in 1569. This started a long series of minor wars which lasted throughout the remainder of the century. Foreign aid was sought and sent in the classic political gambit of the period: Catholic princes were willing to send help to re-conquer the country for the Catholic religion. This was an extension of the principle 'cuius regio, eius religio' (the religion of a country was that of its ruler). The Irish Franciscans living on the Continent were deeply involved. For example, Fr James O'Shea, who carried the papal banner ashore when the Spanish landed near Dingle in July 1579, and Fr Seán O'Farrell, who was hanged at Askeaton in 1587. The rise of the Desmond confederation coincided with the final excommunication of Elizabeth by Pope Pius V in 1570. From then on, the battle between Catholicism and the English authorities became more intense.

A period of almost systematic persecution began. Any friar who had the misfortune to be captured by the English armies was put to death. By the time Queen Elizabeth died as many as thirty-five friars had been killed. The list included such men as Rory MacCongail who, after various escapes, was flogged to death at Armagh in 1565; three friars were captured and killed at Downpatrick in 1575; also Fergal Ward, the guardian of Armagh, was hanged there in the same year and an old friar, Felim O'Hara, was killed before the altar at Moyne because he would not reveal the hiding place of the sacred vessels; Fr John O'Dowd, also of Moyne, was killed in 1579 for not revealing confessional secrets; and in 1585 Fr Donal O'Neillan was thrown a number of times from the top of Trinity Gate, Youghal, and his body used for target practice.

The cause for the canonization of the Irish Martyrs began in Dublin in 1904 and the formal apostolic process on 260 cases opened in 1917. Due to the sheer volume of work, the first stage was not completed until 1978! It was then suggested that a small group should be selected for an immediate process and seventeen were chosen who would have a strong pastoral impact: four bishops (including two Franciscans and a Dominican), two priests, five men and a woman, two Franciscans, an Augustinian, a Dominican and a Jesuit.

The first two Franciscans were Patrick O'Healy, bishop of Mayo, and his companion, Conn O'Rourke, hanged at Kilmallock in mid August 1579. Bishop Patrick was a native of Leitrim who knew the friars at Dromahair. He went to study at the University of Alcalá in Spain before proceeding to Rome. There he took up residence in the friary of Aracoeli before his appointment as bishop in July 1576. It was then papal policy either to leave Irish dioceses under the care of competent priests acting as vicars apostolic, or to ensure that
30 bishops returning to Ireland were imbued with the spirit of the

Counter-Reformation through continental study. In an action typical of the new militant Catholicism, Bishop O'Healy plotted with James Fitzmaurice to return to Ireland with an armed force. They sailed from Lisbon with a handful of men in November 1577 only to be driven back into harbour by storms and have their ship stolen. The bishop continued his journey overland. He stayed with the Franciscans in Paris, impressing them with his learning. There he met a young Franciscan, Conn O'Rourke, one of the O'Rourkes of Breffny. Early in 1579 they set off for Ireland and managed to slip ashore in north Kerry or west Limerick. The bishop was probably still in contact with James Fitzmaurice, whose expeditionary force landed at Dingle in mid-July. In the meantime the two Franciscans made their way to the castle of the earl of Desmond in Askeaton. He was away, but his wife received them and treated them kindly before sending them on their way. She then betrayed them to the authorities. They were arrested and taken to Kilmallock for interrogation. Sir William Drury, who was both lord chief justice and president of Munster, is traditionally said to have supervized their torture. The friars were stripped, flogged, had nails hammered through their fingers and were finally condemned to death without trial because they would not acknowledge Queen Elizabeth I as head of the Church. Then they were hanged, allegedly with the cords from their religious habits. Their bodies were left hanging so that the soldiers could use them for target practice.

One of the Franciscans who accompanied James Fitzmaurice when he landed in Ireland in 1579 was Mateo de Oviedo. He returned a second time with the Spaniards who landed in Smerwick in 1580. Later he became Spanish agent for Hugh O'Neill. He was appointed archbishop of Dublin in 1600, and spent the winter of 1600-1 in Ulster before returning to Spain. He came back to Ireland with del Águila and was with the Spanish forces in Kinsale. He never actually got to Dublin but ruled his diocese through a series of vicars general until his death in 1610. He was a typical product of the Counter-Reformation, willing to fight for his faith by any means available.

This was the period when faith and fatherland became associated in the sense in which they have remained intertwined in Ireland ever since. But the Catholic Church in Ireland was also undergoing reform. Priests trained in the Counter-Reformation tradition on the Continent brought the theology of the Council of Trent to Ireland and the older traditions of the Celtic Church were slowly replaced.

The new friars returning to Ireland were committed to the Counter-Reformation. The plantations in Munster, begun by Catholic Queen Mary, made life in the south of Ireland difficult for

31

the friars. They continued to flourish under Irish protection in the north. The situation worsened under Elizabeth as the policy of plantation developed and the almost continuous warfare after 1570 resulted in the seizure of more friaries. This was especially true during the Nine Years' War waged by O'Neill and O'Donnell. Young men could not be trained in Ireland and it was expensive to go abroad. About five old friaries remained operative, but there were places of refuge all over the country. A new foundation was made at Lisgoole, near Lough Erne in 1583. Training was difficult, but the continental education was excellent. Numbers were low and morale was sagging among the friars when Elizabeth died in 1603. Gaelic life and culture was fading after Kinsale and the Flight of the Earls. Yet in spite of their difficulties, the Irish friars produced a fresh burst of zeal and energy.

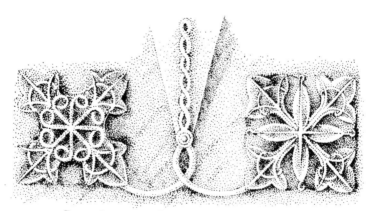

*Decorative carving, Dromahair Friary, Co. Leitrim*

BONAMARGY

STRABANE

CARRICKFERGUS

DONEGAL

ARMAGH          DOWNPATRICK

MOYNE          DROMAHAIR                              DUNDALK

BALLYMOTE          CAVAN

MONS PIETATIS          JAMESTOWN

ELPHIN                                        DROGHEDA

BALLINASAGGART          SLANE

MULTYFARNHAM          TRIM

ROSS          ATHLONE

CLAREGALWAY                    MONASTERORIS          DUBLIN

KILCONNELL          KILLEIGH          CLANE

GALWAY          MEELICK               KILDARE

KINALEHIN                    KILCULLEN

ARAN                    STRADBALLY          WICKLOW

ROSCREA                    BALLINABARBY

ENNIS          NENAGH          CASTLEDERMOT

QUIN

ASKEATON               KILKENNY

LISLAUGHTIN     LIMERICK          DERRYNAFLAN          ENNISCORTHY

ADARE     KILLEEN          CASHEL          NEW ROSS

GALBALLY          CARRICK BEG     WEXFORD

ARDFERT          CLONMEL          WATERFORD

BUTTEVANT

MUCKROSS          YOUGHAL

CORK

KILCREA

BANTRY          TIMOLEAGUE

SHERKIN

34                              *Map III: Franciscan Friaries in Ireland* c. 1650

# Chapter 3

# GOLDEN AGE, REPRESSION AND RENEWAL (1606-1888)

'The history of the Irish Franciscans during the seventeenth century is more glorious than that of any other province.'

Fr Lucian Ceyssens ofm

Despite the persecutions of the Elizabethan era and the defeat of Gaelic Ireland at Kinsale, the Franciscans remained a powerful force in Irish life, at the beginning of the seventeenth century. They would soon be engaged in collecting and preserving the remnants of Gaelic culture and in preaching the new theology of the Counter-Reformation.

Though subject to continued harassment their organization remained vibrant. Every three years the minister general appointed a commissary visitor who presided over a provincial chapter, and the minister provincial elected at chapter went overseas to attend the general chapter. However, the ravages of war had taken their toll: the friaries of Multyfarnham and Donegal were destroyed in 1601-2. The Nine Years' War came to an end with O'Neill's surrender at Mellifont in 1603. The friars hoped that the end of the war, coinciding with the death of Queen Elizabeth I and the accession of the first Stuart monarch, James I, would bring a period of respite. Instead it brought further persecution as the Viceroy, Lord Mountjoy, tried to extend English rule throughout the country. Thus efforts to repossess Catholic churches in Munster and south Leinster were suppressed in the summer of 1603. A proclamation expelling all seminary priests and Jesuits was issued in 1605. Towards the end of that year people petitioning for the private practice of their religion within the Pale were imprisoned. Under these circumstances the provincial chapter due in 1605 could not be held. The outgoing provincial, Edmund O'Mullarkey, accompanied by Owen Friel and some other friars, attended the general chapter of the Order in Toledo at Pentecost 1606.

## Reorganization from Continent in early Seventeenth Century

A major reorganization of the Irish Franciscans began with the appointment of Fr Florence Conry as minister provincial at the Toledo general chapter in 1606. He was born at Cloonahee, County 35

Roscommon *c.* 1560 and educated in the traditional Irish manner. After joining the Franciscans he studied at Salamanca, returning to Ireland with the Spanish forces which landed at Kinsale in 1601. Forced to flee to Spain, he travelled as *anam-chara* of Red Hugh O'Donnell and attended him on his deathbed. His appointment as minister provincial provoked some resentment among the Irish friars who were disappointed at not being allowed to elect a leader. Conry never returned to Ireland, but immediately began to organize the friars along strict Counter-Reformation lines. In particular he organized the first Irish Franciscan continental college, that of St Anthony at Louvain. Here the friars had a base where young men could be properly trained. Many of the early students at Louvain were men who had been studying in colleges for the diocesan clergy, or friars from other parts of Europe. The period of looking back in longing to the past was over. Significantly, it is recorded that at the next provincial chapter in 1609 many Irishmen who had joined other provinces – such as Conry himself had done – were admitted to the Irish province. In 1609 Conry was appointed archbishop of Tuam but remained in Flanders or Spain until his death in 1629.

When the Irish provincial chapter met in 1612, only the friaries of Donegal, Armagh and Multyfarnham had regular communities. The number of guardians in the province was reduced to eight: the above three, Kilconnell, Ross, Limerick, Kilcrea and Waterford. Other houses were given a lesser type of superior called a president and it was decided that discretes would no longer attend chapters because of the danger of travelling. All friars were to live in community and not absent themselves, even for questing, for more than a month. The Franciscan habit was to be worn at all times, albeit as an undergarment when the friar had to travel in disguise. Novices would be trained on the Continent at the new foundation in Louvain.

Prior to the chapter, Conor O'Devaney, bishop of Down and Connor, along with a secular priest, Patrick O'Loughran, was hanged, drawn and quartered in Dublin on 1 February 1612. He is the third Irish Franciscan whose cause for beatification is being actively pursued. Born *c.* 1533, he joined the friars and served in the Donegal community. After his appointment as bishop of Down and Connor in 1582 he took part in a meeting in the diocese of Clogher to promulgate the decrees of the Council of Trent. He was arrested and imprisoned in Dublin Castle 1588-90, but no charge could be made against him, so he was released with a warning. The authorities arrested him again in June 1611 and decided to charge him with consorting with the Ulster Earls before their flight. Fr Patrick was arrested in Cork at the same time. He had returned to Ireland having completed his studies on the Continent. The authorities thought that it would be expedient to execute a bishop, and arranged a show trial at which both priest and bishop were condemned to death. Both went to the gallows steadfastly maintaining their faith. Paradoxically Bishop O'Devaney's death resulted in an improvement in the situation of Catholics in Ireland. His death left only one bishop alive in the country. However, Rome decided that the time had come to make new appointments.

At the next chapter, held in Waterford on 18 September 1615, Fr Donagh Mooney was elected provincial by unanimous vote. A man of boundless energy, he rejuvenated Franciscan life in Ireland once again. He was greatly helped in this task by such men as Florence Conry and Luke Wadding. The chapter issued statutes on many matters. Preaching was re-organized, and a strict examination for faculties was introduced. Eight friars were admitted to the Irish province from other provinces while six were expelled.

Donagh Mooney was born near Ballymore c. 1577 and, possibly after a brief military career, joined the Franciscans in October 1600. Before he could finish his novitiate, Donegal friary was destroyed and he was transferred to Multyfarnham. Two days before his profession, the Irish provincial, Fr John Grey, was captured with some other friars. In order to make his profession Br Donagh Mooney let himself be captured and took his Franciscan vows imprisoned in the same cell with the minister provincial! He escaped in a matter of days and acted as guardian of Armagh at a chapter held in woods near Leitrim. Ordained at Dromahair, he went to France to complete his studies and was appointed the first guardian of the new college at Louvain in 1606-7. On his return to Ireland he was stationed in Drogheda. He later became second-in-command of the Irish Franciscans before being elected provincial in 1615. He wrote an account of his visitation of all friaries in Ireland, which was probably composed at Louvain while on his way to the general chapter of the Order at Salamanca in 1618. He added some historical notes later and the result, the *Tractatus de Provincia Hiberniae*, is a major source for Irish Franciscan history. Donagh Mooney died at Drogheda in April 1624. During his term of office, small residences were established at Cavan, Clonmel, Dublin, Kinalehin, Limerick, Lisgoole, New Ross and Wexford. By the end of his period as provincial, there were some one hundred and twenty friars in Ireland (of whom thirty-three were approved preachers), a start had been made on a permanent building in Louvain and this college had already sent about twenty-five trained priests back to Ireland.

The strength and tenacity of the Franciscan Order at the time is summed up in a report which the archbishop of Dublin sent to Rome in 1623:

... to these must be added about two hundred Franciscans, who are especially to be commended, because they never suffered themselves to become extinct in the kingdom, and were the only religious who maintained the fight in some districts ...

Though there had been many arrests during the early part of the century, few of those imprisoned were put to death.

A provincial chapter held in Limerick in 1629 was the first for which the full chapter bill is extant. It nearly ended in disaster when the drunken behaviour of some of the 'hangers-on' attracted the attention of the city authorities. While there had been only eight guardianates in 1612, superiors could now be appointed to houses in: Limerick, Cork, Quin, Sherkin, Timoleague, Kilcrea, Youghal, Cashel, Clonmel, Waterford, New Ross, Wexford, Kilkenny, Kildare, Dublin, Multyfarnham, Athlone, Drogheda, Cavan, Dundalk, Lisgoole, Armagh, Carrickfergus, Down, Donegal, Dromahair, Moyne, Ross, Kinalehin, Galway, Kilconnell and Trim. Special arrangements were made for Muckross and Lislaughtin. Appointments were also made for the continental colleges, but this had to be done in a rather complicated manner. Twenty-five houses were listed as vacant. This chapter showed the steady progress which had been made. It was followed by one of those periods of mild persecution typical of the century and usually coinciding with a change of viceroy. However, this only slightly retarded the expansion of the friars during these years.

The problem of training young Franciscans for work in Ireland was solved by the opening of houses in Catholic countries on the Continent. Individual friars had been educated outside Ireland for many years. The obvious choice for the site of the first Irish Franciscan continental college was Louvain (now officially Leuven) in Belgium. On a well-known trade route, it was the site of a famous university and was in a country governed by militantly Catholic Spain. The College of St Anthony was founded there in 1606, and moved to its present site in 1617. Fr Luke Wadding, again with some Spanish help, founded St Isidore's College in Rome. Most of the first community arrived from Louvain on 21 June 1625. Fr Malachy Fallon was sent eastwards from Louvain in 1629 to seek another foundation. His mission resulted in the College of the Immaculate Conception at Prague which was officially opened on 6 July 1631. Sympathetic Polish friars gave the Irish the use of a friary at Wielun for a number of years. Further efforts produced a temporary residence at Paris, but foundations at Jablonow (Poland) and Namslav (Silesia) were unsuccessful. From Rome, a novitiate was opened at Capranica in 1656.

38    These colleges, and the later foundation at Boulay, provided a

steady flow of priests until most of them were closed at the time of the French Revolution. On average ten friars returned from the Continent each year. Prague, with a capacity of up to one hundred friars, provided five or six new priests each year; Louvain with a capacity of forty provided two or three; Rome was similar to Louvain. Clerical training was fairly rigorous: a year's novitiate in Ireland or on the Continent, followed by four years of philosphy and theology on the Continent during which there was constant training in preaching and casuistry in both Irish and English, and ending with exams on returning to Ireland. Initially discipline in the colleges was strict, although abuses did creep in at a later stage. Without these colleges, the Irish friars would have ceased to exist. But not all training was carried out on the Continent. In the 1620s secondary schools were opened by the friars in Drogheda, Dundalk and Wexford. Houses of philosophy started in Cashel, Drogheda, Dublin, Galway, Kilkenny, Multyfarnham and Timoleague, as well as a house of theology in Dublin. This latter house had a very short life due to persecution, but several of the others flourished for years and supplied students to the continental colleges.

In this period provincialism became important. Each of the continental colleges became associated to some extent with friars from one particular area: Prague for the Leinstermen, Louvain for the Ulstermen and Connachtmen, Rome for the Munstermen, Paris for the Catholics of Old English descent. Each of the four definitors (the assistants to the provincial) had to be from a different province. The provincial also came from each province in turn. This practice of rotating provincials and definitors continued until the middle of the nineteenth century.

In 1623 an effort was made to split the Irish province into two on a racial basis: Munster-Leinster (for the Old English) and Ulster-Connacht (for the Gaelic Irish). The provincial chapter at Athlone in 1644 requested a formal division into two provinces. This was approved by the general chapter at Toledo in 1645, but was rejected by the provincial chapter at Ross in 1647. Except for a brief resurrection at the chapter at Buttevant in 1673, the matter was allowed to die quietly. However, the spirit of provincialism remained alive. An Italian friar, visitator of the Irish province, said that outside his civil province of origin, the provincial was like a foreigner in another country (*un Provinciale forastiero di lontan paese*).

The structure of the Franciscan Order on the Continent had been re-organized during the sixteenth century. About 1526 the office of commissary of the German-Belgian Nation was created. The commissary had authority over most of the provinces in Germany, those in Belgium and also those in England and Ireland. When he began to exercise his authority over the Irish friars is uncertain, but he played a part in the foundation of St Anthony's College, Louvain, in 1606.

In 1633 General Statutes were approved by which the General Constitutions adopted at the general chapter at Segovia in 1621 were adapted to the needs of the German-Belgian nation. These Statutes remained the basic law for the Irish Franciscans until the end of the nineteenth century. The standard interpretation used was that of a Belgian friar named Kerchove.

In the mid-seventeenth century, the Irish province took the name Recollect. This title, and membership of the German-Belgian nation, were of little practical importance in the life of the Irish friars, except for a brief period in the mid-nineteenth century.

Young priests returning to Ireland in the first half of the seventeenth century joined communities living fairly openly despite the persecution. In Drogheda, for example, four priests lived in a rented house, each with his own room, but with a common kitchen and refectory. The habit was worn within the house, but on the few occasions when the friars went out they wore secular clothes. There was a small but select library, and the community meditated and recited the divine office in choir behind the main altar of the church. This was a separate building with a fixed altar, a pulpit and confessionals. In other places, such as Dublin, there were side altars, paintings and statues. Masses were celebrated regularly each day, and a priest was on duty for counselling and confessions. Confraternities such as the Cordbearers of St Francis, as well as the Franciscan Third Order, met regularly. It is clear that preaching missions, sometimes associated with questing, also flourished.

## Literary Activities

The Golden Age of the Irish Franciscans is mainly associated with their outstanding literary output. Initially this was centred on Louvain, concentrating on Irish culture, but gradually the writings of the Irish friars at Rome and Prague became prominent, with an increased emphasis on Franciscanism and on theology.

The Louvain school is best known for the activities of Br Micheál Ó Cléirigh, compiler, with Fearfeasa Ó Maolconaire, Cúcoigcríche Ó Duibhgeannáin and Cúcoigcríche Ó Cléirigh, of the *Annals of the Four Masters*. Completed in 1637, it was not printed until 1851. As a result of his work and that of other friars of the Louvain school, there is still a large collection of Irish manuscripts in Brussels. He also wrote *Foclóir, nó Sanasán Nua*, as well as helping in the compilation of the *Réim Ríoghraidhe na hÉireann agus Senchas a Naomh*.

40     The first known Irish grammar, *Rudimenta Grammaticae Hibernicae*,

*Title-page of* An Teagasg Críosdaidhe *(Antwerp 1611). This catechism by Fr Bonaventure O'Hussey was the first book to be printed in an Irish font.*

and the first Irish catechism, which was also the first book printed in an Irish font, *Teagasg Críosdaidhe* (Antwerp 1611, later reprinted at Louvain and in Rome), were the work of Fr Bonaventure O'Hussey. The catechism was one of a number of books produced in Louvain in order to educate Irish Catholics in Counter-Reformation theology. As one friar wrote: '*Nach do mhúnadh Gaoidhilge sgríobhmaoid ach do mhúnadh na haithridhe*'. Florence Conry's *Desiderius*; Antoine Gearon's *Parrthas an Anma*; Aodh MacAingil's *Scáthán Shacramuinte na hAithridhe*, are among the other books produced at Louvain.

Fr Florence Conry, the founder of St Anthony's College, had studied St Augustine and was a friend of Cornelius Jansens, with whom he engaged in theological dialogue. He was much respected by the early Jansenists. His works include: *Doctrine of Grace according to St Augustine, Tractatus de statu parvulorum*, and *Tractatus de Augustini sensu . . . B.V.M. Conceptionem*. Notes made by Fr Luke Wadding in Rome are also a major source for the history of Jansenism.

In Rome Fr Luke Wadding prepared an edition of the writings of     41

St Francis. His main effort went into organizing the monumental *Annales Ordinis Minorum* – envizaged as a comprehensive history of the Franciscans – and the *Scriptores Ordinis Minorum* – a complete list of Franciscan authors. Wadding was also the inspiration behind the first critical edition of Duns Scotus (Lyons, 1639 ss.), although most of the work was done by John Punch, Anthony Hickey and Aodh MacAingil.

Other important Irish Franciscan works of the period include: Francis Molloy's *Lucerna Fidelium* – another Irish catechism; the work of Fr John Colgan on the lives of the Irish saints – *Acta Sanctorum Hiberniae* (1645) – and *Triadis Thaumaturgae* (1647); the summary histories of the Irish Franciscans prepared by Fr Donagh Mooney and also by Fr Francis Matthews; the works of Fr Maurice Conry and of Fr Anthony Broudin on the lives of the Irish martyrs; the *Collectanea Sacra* of Fr Patrick Fleming; the *Summa Theologica* of Francis Bermingham; and the *Roma Triumphans Septicollis* of Raymond Caron. The complete edition of the works of Fr Bonaventure Baron came to twenty-two volumes. This is just a small selection of the material which made the seventeenth century the Golden Age of the Irish Franciscans.

## The Confederation of Kilkenny and Cromwellian Persecution

Expansion continued during the 1630s until there were communities in forty seven houses. When war broke out again in 1641 ten houses remained vacant. But there were some six hundred members in the province and a strong continental system of support was in place. The strongly Catholic atmosphere of the times encouraged further expansion. New foundations were made in such unpromising places as Jamestown in Protestant mid-Leitrim and Ballinabarny in desolate south Wicklow. Some neglected Third Order foundations were revived as First Order houses – Ballinasaggart, Ballymote, Killeenagallive, possibly Killedan/Mons Pietatis. By 1646, there was a total of sixty-two communities.

During the 1640s the friars on the Continent became involved politically in the affairs of the Confederation. Fr Francis O'Sullivan arranged for the transport of supplies from Spain, Fr James FitzSimons acted as a secret agent in London and Fr Luke Wadding was an important Irish influence in Rome.

Just as the politicians in the Confederation were divided in their basic loyalties, so also the friars were divided between loyalty to Rinuccini, the Papal Nuncio, or to the duke of Ormond, the commander of the Royalist forces. The majority of the friars remained loyal to the Nuncio, possibly remembering the part played by Luke Wadding in bringing him to Ireland. The provincial chapter of 1648 had to be held under the protection of Owen Roe O'Neill, since the Ormondists wished to halt it. The bitter internal dispute between the friars faded with the arrival of Oliver Cromwell at Dublin in 1649. Significantly, the semi-national synod which condemned Ormond in 1650 was held in the friary at Jamestown. The division within the friars, which reflected the national division between Irish and Old English, was submerged until the Restoration.

The friars suffered heavily under Cromwell. Within a year of his arrival as many as ten friars had been killed, including the Franciscan bishop of Elphin, Dr Boetius Egan. He was captured by troops involved in the siege of Clonmel and was hanged and dismembered near Macroom. During 1651 another ten friars were killed. Details are scant as the friars had gone underground and ceased to keep records. In so far as they were able, they continued to minister in the areas around the old friaries, but the buildings themselves were often taken over by the Cromwellian authorities. Kilcrea, for example, was garrisoned by troops during the early 1650s. Individual friars were pursued relentlessly and killed when caught: for example Fr Eugene O'Cahan, a well-known lecturer of philosophy and theology during his years in Italy, was captured in north Kerry, released, re-captured in north Cork and killed in 1652.

The fourth Irish Franciscan whose beatification is being actively considered is Fr John Kearney, hanged at Clonmel on 21 March 1653. A native of Cashel, he was born in 1619 and was received into the Franciscan novitiate in Kilkenny in 1635-6. After his profession he went to study at St Anthony's College, Louvain, and set out for Ireland shortly after his ordination in September 1642. He was captured at sea by English Parliamentarians and taken from Bristol to London, where he was imprisoned, tortured and condemned to death. On the eve of his execution he escaped to France with the help of an English Catholic and was later able to reach Ireland through Calais and Wexford. He spent two years teaching philosophy in Cashel before going on to Waterford as master of novices. His mother was among those slaughtered by Inchiquin in Cashel cathedral in September 1647. The arrival of Cromwell forced him to flee from Waterford in 1649. The following year he was appointed guardian of the friary of Carrick-on-Suir and continued ministering in the Suir valley despite the persecution. In March 1652 he was captured at Cashel and sent to Clonmel. At his trial, he proclaimed that he was a Franciscan priest whose duty it was to say Mass and administer the sacraments. He was hanged in his religious habit and his body brought back for burial in the chapter hall of the ruined friary in Cashel.

On 6 January 1653 the Commissioners for Irish affairs of the

English Parliament issued an edict banishing all 'persons in Popish Orders' and even provided ships for those who wished to go. With over forty friars dead, some of those remaining in the country chose exile. A number went to the continental colleges, but many settled wherever they landed. When Fr Isaac Horan ofm was returning to Louvain in the autumn of 1653 with the remains of Dr Florence Conry, the founder of St Anthony's College, he met three Irish friars in a tiny fishing village in Castille. Many priests became chaplains to Irish regiments in foreign armies; there were eight of them with the Spanish army in Flanders in 1654. A few settled in other Franciscan provinces and the minister general had to issue regulations to force them to correspond in civilized Latin. They had been writing letters in Irish and the continentals were suspicious of their contents.

Some friars remained in Ireland. Fr John Dalton ofm was the only priest in Kilkenny at the time of his capture on the Feast of the Portiuncula in 1653. Hanged and quartered on 5 August, he was the last friar to fall victim to the Cromwellians. Five pounds remained the reward for information about a priest. Two camps were set up, one on Aran, the other on Inishbofin, to house captured priests. Transportation, particularly to the Barbadoes, was quite common. Despite all this, the friars continued their work in many parts of the country.

By 1658 the situation had eased sufficiently to enable the friars to hold a provincial chapter at Ballinasaggart. Fr Bernard Egan was elected provincial, but such was the uncertainty of the times that four others were nominated to succeed him, if necessary. Superiors were appointed for some thirty friaries, mainly in the midlands, the west and the north east. By 1661 all friaries seem to have been restored. There was an estimated total of two hundred friars in Ireland and one hundred and fifty on the Continent. The friars were aided in their work by the extensive faculties granted them by Pope Paul V in 1612 and again by Pope Alexander VII in 1655.

## The Restoration: A Troubled Period

The years following the accession of King Charles II were difficult ones for the Catholic Church in Ireland. It took some time for the hierarchy to be re-vitalized. Unsavoury rows broke out between priests and religious over rights. One of the most infamous of these was between the Franciscans and the Dominicans in Ulster in which St Oliver Plunkett played a major role. The underlying cause of these difficulties was the lack of sufficient money to support the clergy.

Most damaging for the Franciscans was the re-emergence of the Nuncio/Ormond split in the activities of Fr Peter Walsh ofm. His
activities are best summed up in a phrase 'An Irish Gallican Inter-

lude', since the point at issue was civil control of Church affairs. The Restoration of Charles II in May 1660 had raised Catholic hopes. Fr Walsh was appointed Irish Catholic agent in London in January 1661. The previous month some laymen in Dublin, mainly Old English, had drafted a formula of loyalty which contained a statement of grievances, a petition for protection, and a protestation of allegiance (afterwards known as the Remonstrance). With the help of Ormond (now Lord Lieutenant), Fr Walsh began to seek support for the formula in Ireland by all the means at his disposal. Eventually Ormond arranged a national synod to be held in Dublin in June 1666. This special synod would only accept a modified version of the formula. Ormond then tried to get the Franciscan Order to accept it, since the friars were meeting in provincial chapter. In the ensuing confusion the chapter had to be adjourned. Fr Walsh fought on, writing much in defence of his own viewpoint. Although excommunicated in 1670, he submitted shortly before his death in 1688.

Another famous Franciscan of the period was Fr James Taaffe ofm, who was appointed visitator of Ireland by the papal authorities in 1666. The exact terms of his appointment are unclear, but it seems that he was not granted the special faculties which he considered necessary. On his arrival in Ireland in March 1668 after a delay of two years, he claimed the title of apostolic visitator and commissary general of the Irish Church. He tried to rectify the tangled problems of Church jurisdiction, which had become chaotic following fifteen years without proper episcopal supervision. His decisions were so unpopular that nearly all of them were appealed to Rome. In 1671 Fr Taaffe himself arrived back in Rome, was fully absolved from all censures and the whole incident was quietly forgotten.

The activities of Taaffe and Walsh delayed the re-organization of the Irish friars. Rome appointed Fr Peter Gaynor as vicar provincial in 1669. He was able to appoint superiors to fifty-six friaries, leaving seven vacant. A full chapter was held at Elphin in 1672. By then there were sufficient friars in Ireland to appoint superiors for all the houses in the country. Re-organization continued even during the periods of renewed persecution in 1673-4 and in 1678 during the Titus Oates plot.

St Oliver Plunkett is the best-known Irish victim of the Titus Oates plot. Another of its victims was an Irish Franciscan, the Blessed Charles Meehan. He was born c. 1650 in the Leitrim area. After joining the Franciscans at St Anthony's College, Louvain, he was ordained between 1670 and 1672. Having studied in Louvain for a number of years he went to Hammelburg in Bavaria in 1674 and then to St Isidore's College, Rome, in 1676. While studying he was able to support himself through mass stipends and stole fees. Early in 1678 he set out to return to Ireland. That summer he was shipwrecked off the coast of England or Wales, and arrested but later released. He resumed his journey, this time going overland towards Conway, then the point of embarkation for boats to Ireland. In late June 1678 he was arrested at Denbigh in north Wales on suspicion of being a popish priest. The matter was referred to London for a ruling, but administrative confusion delayed a reply. At this point it was not illegal to be a Catholic priest in England, but only to minister as a priest. Fr Charles had been very careful about this matter and had not ministered. He was therefore very frustrated at his continued detention. On 28 September 1678 Titus Oates revealed details of an imaginary 'Popish plot' to the authorities in London. The next day the local justices began to prepare the book of evidence against Fr Meehan. Throughout the winter of 1678-9 raids and arrests in connection with the Oates plot continued. Although some of those implicated by Oates were tried during the winter, most trials occurred early in the following spring. Fr Meehan was brought to trial at Ruthin on 28 April 1679, charged with treason. His confession that he was a Catholic priest was considered sufficient to condemn him and his pleas that he had observed the law were ignored. He was sentenced to death and the matter referred to London. Though the hysteria caused by the plot had begun to abate, executions were still being carried out. On the morning of 12 August 1679 Fr Meehan was taken from his cell in Ruthin and dragged on a wooden sled through the streets to the place of execution where he made his final speech: He was proud to be a priest, he had kept the law, he prayed for those who condemned him and finally for the conversion of Charles II. He was then hanged, drawn and quartered. He was beatified by Pope John Paul II on 22 November 1987.

Following the coronation of James II in 1685, the friars expected greater tolerance for the Catholic religion. The provincial chapter at Ross in 1687 appointed superiors to fifty-six houses in Ireland. Most of these were staffed by friars trained in the continental colleges.

In the new atmosphere of hope the friars tried to reconstruct some churches. Work began in Athlone in 1687 but was never completed due to the Jacobite war. In Dublin the friars returned to the site of their mediaeval foundation and built a small church eighty feet by twenty. The altar-piece, four pillars and steps were of Kilkenny marble, the floor was flagged and there was a shrine to St Anthony. But the respite was to be short-lived.

## The Penal Laws

46 After the battle of the Boyne, King William III was willing to treat

Catholics with toleration. However, English politics and politicians dictated otherwise. The 'Banishment of Religious Act' was passed in 1697. Hopes that the royal assent would be refused proved groundless, and the Act came into force in May 1698. Meeting in Dublin on the 15 February, the provincial definitory had decided to obey the Act in principle. Goods would be given into safe keeping, novices sent to the Continent, while permission would be sought for the old and infirm friars to remain in Ireland. A survey in 1700 gives the first set of reliable statistics for the Irish Franciscans: four hundred and twenty priests, fifty-four brothers, nineteen students and sixteen novices – a total of five hundred and nine friars. The direct and indirect effects of persecution would reduce this total to about one hundred and fifty friars by 1782.

Many friars obeyed the Act of Banishment by going to live on the Continent. With the help of the duke of Lorraine, a new college was founded at Boulay, near Metz, in 1698. The following year the pope was reputedly helping to support two hundred and fourteen Irish friars in French territory. However, many of the friars settled in the existing Irish continental colleges. A number obtained posts as military chaplains with various armies. Fr Charles Fleming ofm was accidentally shot by a firing-squad while absolving a deserter at Gravelines in 1739; Fr John Clarke ofm was reputedly with the Irish at Fontenoy in 1745; Fr Bonaventure O'Donoghue was with the French army in Louisiana in 1718. Many friars sailed the seas as naval chaplains. Some became chaplains to overseas colonists, for example Fr Gabriel Cullinan served as chaplain to the settlers in Haiti for fifteen years after 1739; James Dease died in Calcutta in 1757 while serving as a chaplain there.

The Franciscans who remained in Ireland found that the application of the new law was rather spasmodic. The ex-provincial fled to Louvain and some of the provincial administration was carried out from Flanders, where the middle chapter of 1669 and the provincial chapter of 1700 were held. The provincial archives were moved to St Anthony's College, Louvain. The situation had improved sufficiently to hold the middle chapter of 1702 in Co. Cavan and the provincial chapter of 1703 in Dublin. Yet in 1714 it again proved impossible to hold the provincial chapter because of harassment. This was also the period of the priest-catcher. Initially the most famous was Edward Tyrell, who betrayed Paul Byrne, curate in Howth and probably a Franciscan, in 1710. Lady Howth secured the friar's release. After Tyrell was hanged for bigamy, a Spanish Jew called John Garzia appeared. He inveigled the Franciscans in Cook St, Dublin, into giving him shelter, then betrayed three of them, along with the archbishop of Dublin and three others, in June 1718. One friar was

47

A  *Nave*
B  *Choir*
C  *Aisle*
D  *Chapel*
E  *Sacristy*
F  *Transept*
G  *Cloister Garth*
H  *Tower*
I  *West Doorway*
J  *Chapter House*
K  *Kitchen*
L  *Dormitory*
M  *Residence*
N  *Refectory*
P  *Day Room*

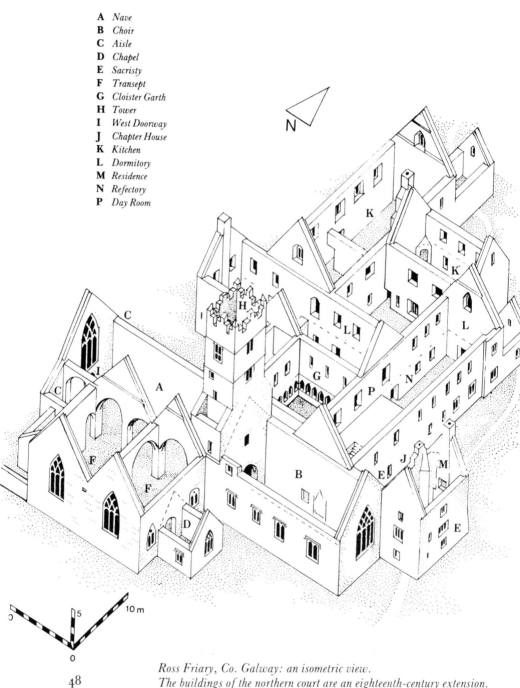

10 m

*Ross Friary, Co. Galway: an isometric view.*
*The buildings of the northern court are an eighteenth-century extension.*

sent into exile in Spain, another was sentenced to exile but seems to have escaped, while a third languished in prison for several years. However, by 1720 the friars had begun to emerge from their places of hiding. Thus from 1723 on the friars in Galway were saying mass in public, yet the mayor could find nobody there when he raided the place!

This highlights an important aspect of eighteenth century life in Ireland: what was seen to happen was more important than what was actually done. Endless reports on the state of popery were produced and analysed. Sheriffs sent in details of arrests, but very often the priests concerned vanished before being brought to trial. Titles such as lector jubilate or senior discrete became important. Even within the Order life was highly structured. In the 1730s the students in the College of the Immaculate Conception in Prague were living in very poor conditions, while their superiors and lecturers were living in luxury. Such double standards lasted at least until the French Revolution.

One method of evading the law was to register as diocesan priests, since the persecution was directed more against bishops and religious than against the parochial clergy. As early as 1714, the provincial chapter had to lay down rules for friars acting as diocesan clergy. Many Franciscans took charge of parishes near their old friaries. Others took over large areas, especially in south Ulster and the midlands, where they carried on widespread pastoral activity. For example the friars at Multyfarnham served that parish while living in a small cottage from c. 1705 until 1804. The friars of Trim served an extensive area around Courtown from c. 1720 to 1826. Most of the diocese of Clonmacnois was served by the Franciscans, particularly Athlone from 1723 to 1766. The friars also served numerous parishes in Kilmore diocese, a few in Raphoe and several in south Armagh. The friars of Monaghan town worked in parts of south Monaghan. While the friars moved into parish work in a number of larger towns, an unusual system evolved in Wexford, Waterford and Clonmel by which they helped the parochial clergy by working in the parish church while living in their own house. A great deal of research remains to be done on eighteenth-century parish history in Ireland, and we are only now beginning to realize the extent of Franciscan involvement.

Due to their continental training, and Franciscan influence at the court-in-exile of the Stuarts at St Germain, where Fr Bernard Kelly ofm was chaplain and secretary to the Young Pretender, many friars were appointed bishops in Ireland. In Killala: Dr Thadeus Francis O'Rourke (1707-36), Dr Peter Archdeken (1736-9), Dr Bonaventure McDonnell (1749-60). In Dromore: Dr Denis Maguire (1767-70),  49 who was translated to Kilmore (1770-93), Dr Patrick Brady (1770-80). In Down and Connor: Dr James O'Shiel (1717-24), Dr Francis Stuart (1740-51). In Ferns: Dr Ambrose O'Callaghan (1729-44). In Killaloe: Dr Sylvester Lloyd (1729-39), who was translated to Waterford and Lismore (1739-47). He had edited an Irish catechism while staying with the English Franciscans at Douai.

In an effort to maintain their numbers, the friars began to admit novices in various houses even though the canonical requirements for a novitiate could not be completely fulfilled. It became customary to ordain candidates to the priesthood before they began their studies. Such young men could proceed to one of the colleges on the Continent and support themselves, at least partially, by accepting stipends for masses and other services. The bishops used a similar system to train Irish diocesan priests.

This practice was open to abuse and eventually Rome decided to act. Fr John Kent (President of the Irish Pastoral College at Louvain) was sent to investigate in 1742. For the diocesan clergy, it was eventually decided to impose the obligation of residence on the bishops and to limit the number of priests they might ordain. For religious in general, and the friars in particular, a set of decrees was promulgated by Propaganda Fide in Rome in 1751: novices could only be received in houses of regular life on the Continent and needed the permission of the Nuncio at Brussels before they could return to Ireland on completion of their studies – furthermore, a bishop had the power of veto over the movement of religious from his diocese. These decrees were an over-reaction to undoubted abuses. They stifled religious life in Ireland, and the numerical strength of the friars began to decline. A fall in numbers of diocesan clergy prompted a greater involvement of religious in running parishes. This eventually caused tension between the diocesan and regular clergy, especially towards the end of the century.

The decrees of 1751 soon began to take effect. Appeals to Rome commenced and as a result we have a very good summary of the state of the Irish Franciscans in 1766. There were regular friaries at or near: Dublin, Kilkenny, Athlone, Multyfarnham, Wexford, Trim, Youghal, Cork, Waterford, Ennis, Limerick, Clonmel, Buttevant, Carrickbeg, Quin, Claregalway, Galway, Kilconnell, Elphin, Ross, Meelick, Kinalehin, Drogheda, Armagh-Dungannon. However, the communities were quite small, usually numbering only two or three friars. The overall total was one hundred and nine, of whom about half were sick or elderly. There were about seventy-five friars working in parishes, as well as about thirty-five working outside of Ireland. This gives an approximate total of two hundred and twenty, compared with about five hundred and fifty during the first half of the century. By 1782 numbers had dropped to about one hundred and fifty. Rome relented somewhat in 1773, but the damage had already been done. Numbers continued to fall throughout the next century, reaching an all-time low of about seventy-five by 1890.

## Relief and Revolution: The Later Eighteenth Century

The intermittent persecutions during the first half of the century, and the falling numbers of friars after the 1760s, meant that the second half of the eighteenth century was a difficult time for the Irish Franciscans. Morale plummeted. A few conformed to the Established Church, including Anthony Burke who became a preacher at St Patrick's Cathedral, Dublin, in 1758. There were student riots in St Isidore's College in Rome. That college became bankrupt in 1782 and was only saved when Rome removed its superiors and placed it under direct control. Even at such a low point the Franciscans could still produce friars who were able to take control of the situation and restore the fortunes of the province, notably the McCormick brothers in Rome.

During the early part of the eighteenth century the friars worked in small, well-hidden, chapels or oratories where a hundred people at the most could gather. In the second half of the century they became more public in their activities and began to build new churches. The friars of Dublin were among the first, opening a new chapel in 1749. The existing chapel was so poor that part of it had collapsed in 1716. The new structure was highly decorated with a painting of the Crucifixion over the high altar, and paintings of the Assumption and the Annunciation on either side. There was a pulpit and a side-altar, with one gallery for the choir and another for part of the congregation. Pickpockets were a major problem, as were beggars blocking the doors on Sundays. The friars in Cork built a new church in 1771 and those in Limerick in 1782-3. In Wexford a new church was opened in 1690 and remained in use because it was also the parish church. It underwent major reconstruction in 1781-90.

Much of this activity was a result of political changes which had improved the position of Catholics in Ireland in the later eighteenth century. Most significant was the Relief Act of 1782. This enabled the friars to work with greater freedom and to take on fresh apostolates. The Franciscans hoped that they would now be free to lead a full religious and pastoral life. They hoped that they could also receive novices in Ireland. Yet these hopes were to be frustrated by the direct and indirect effects of the French Revolution. The continental colleges were closed. The Irish Franciscans had come to depend very much on these colleges. While a small number of men were admitted to the novitiate in Ireland, most aspirants to the Order were sent to the Continent for their novitiate and to complete their studies.

The first act which adversely affected the continental colleges was the religious policy of Joseph II of the Austro-Hungarian Empire. Prague was closed in 1786 due to his decisions, although some Irish friars remained active in the area until after the Napoleonic period. Louvain was kept open for a time despite attempts to close it. In the maelstrom of the French Revolution, Boulay was closed in 1792 and Louvain the following year. Rome and Capranica were closed for longer or shorter periods, but were operating again by 1818. The friars were forced to open a novitiate, as well as houses of philosophy and theology, in Ireland. The principal centres were Wexford and Cork. Due to doubt about the future of the colleges on the Continent, the Irish friars made arrangements for a number of young men to go to Spain for their novitiate and studies between 1817 and 1833. By 1815 it was obvious that Prague was permanently lost. Some efforts were made to re-open Boulay. Even the Trojan work of Fr Cowan ofm failed to restore St Anthony's College in Louvain as an Irish Franciscan college. While the English Franciscans became virtually extinct due to the loss of their college at Douai, the Irish friars survived thanks to their two houses in Italy.

A major sign of the new religious tolerance in Ireland was the opening of St Patrick's College, Maynooth, in 1795. There were, of course, political motives behind the British government's decision to support its foundation, principally the desire to cut off the Irish clergy from the contaminating influence of continental revolutionary ideas. The first Professor of Scripture at Maynooth was an Irish Franciscan, Fr Thomas Clancy, who had been lecturing in Prague. Appointed in 1795, he resigned in 1797 to return to, and die in, his beloved Prague. The rise of Maynooth and the other Irish seminaries meant more diocesan clergy were available for parish duties. This left less scope for pastoral activity by the friars.

In 1800 the friars were still at work in or near their old houses at Dublin, Wexford, Cashel (= Thurles), Claregalway, Athlone, Youghal, Limerick, Galway, Multyfarnham, Waterford, Clonmel, Meelick, Cork, Ennis, Carrickbeg, Drogheda and Ross; then Quin (= Drim), Dungannon, Trim, Jamestown, Buttevant, St John Baptist (= Edgeworthston), Timoleague, Galbally (= Mitchelstown), Elphin, Killeigh, Monaghan, Cavan, Lisgoole, Donegal and about six other areas in Ulster. Of these thirty-seven sites, the friars were still resident at only the first seventeen by 1830. There had been about seventy friars engaged in parish work in 1800, and this number had fallen to about five in 1830. One or two friars continued to be involved in parish work up to the 1860s when the Franciscans handed over the parish of Aglish, the last place of refuge of the friars of Youghal, following the death of Fr Pat Lonergan in 1862.

The withdrawal of the friars from parish work was not without its problems. The most notorious of these was a dispute between the bishop of Cork and the four religious orders in the city about the obligation of religious to preach in the cathedral. This dispute lasted for nearly thirty years until two decrees were issued from Rome in 1815. Further disputes, particularly that in Waterford in 1834-5, concerned the rights of the friars to have public churches rather than serving in parish churches.

The long line of Franciscan bishops in Ireland came to an end with Dr Patrick Maguire (coadjutor to Dr O'Reilly of Kilmore, 1818-26, but outlived by Dr O'Reilly). When, in 1821, Dr Touhy of Limerick requested, to the delight of many, that Fr William O'Meara ofm be appointed his coadjutor, a strong clerical minority within the diocese objected so vehemently that Rome refused the request.

## Franciscan Life in Ireland during the Emancipation Era

For most of the nineteenth century, the friars lived and dressed as diocesan priests. They had house-keepers and servants to look after them. Brothers were practically unknown, although there were a number of perpetual tertiaries who did house work. Their principal pastoral role was the provision of advice and counselling. If the friars had a church of their own, it was usually small. In the first quarter of the century many friary churches were rebuilt, for example, Carrickbeg and Athlone, sometimes on a new site such as Limerick or on the mediaeval site as at Clonmel. Income came from stipends, questing (done after mass on Sundays), alms and a little manual work (especially market-gardening). Each friar looked after his own needs and there was no such thing as a community purse. Certain expenses, for instance the wages of servants and the provincial tax for the support of St Isidore's in Rome, were paid jointly. Food and drink were matters for the individual. Typically these men had the Franciscan qualities of gentleness, kindness and courtesy to all, and were men of principle.

Formation usually began with a year's novitiate in Ireland. Cork was the principal centre in the early nineteenth century, but was later replaced by Wexford. Solemn vows were taken immediately after the novitiate, since the period of simple profession was only introduced in 1856. After the novitiate the cleric went to Rome for three or four years of study. Having entered the Order about the age of sixteen, he was usually ordained about the age of twenty.

The administrative structure of the Irish province at this time was rather loose. The provincial continued to live in the house where he had formerly resided. Of the ten provincials during the Revolutio-

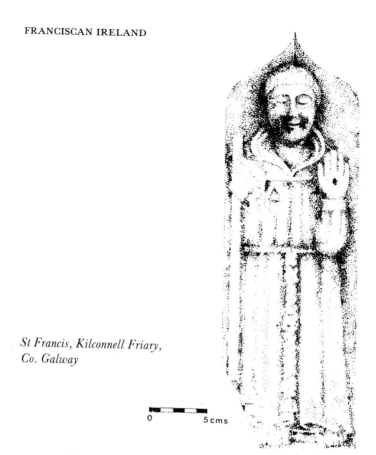

*St Francis, Kilconnell Friary,*
*Co. Galway*

0          5 cms

nary period (1788-1822), two each were based in Drogheda and Cork, one each in Dublin and Wexford, two were parish priests, one in Elphin, the other in London, one lived somewhere in south Ulster and the last lived in Belgium. The positions of provincial, custos and definitors were still strictly rotated by civil province and continued so despite a decree of Propaganda Fide forbidding this practice in 1819. Provincial or intermediate chapters were held every three years, although this was extended to four years for a while due to the difficulty of maintaining regular contact with Rome during the Napoleonic wars. An Irish friar nominated by the minister general on the recommendation of the previous chapter usually presided. As the continuing decline in vocations forced the closure of houses, titular guardians were appointed over these friaries.

When the restrictions on the friars were eased in the early 1800s, one of the new apostolates which they took up was education. Schools were run by the First Order for varying periods during the century in such places as Athlone, Carrickbeg, Clonmel, Dalkey, Killarney, Limerick, Multyfarnham and Wexford. Since there was such a small number of friars in each community, they had to employ lay teachers to help staff these schools. The present 'Monks of the West' (Third Order Brothers of Mountbellew) originated in this fashion.

Given the conditions and spirit of the age it was natural for the more energetic friars to become involved in politics. Fr Denis Taaffe is reputed to have commanded a company of the insurgents in 1798. Of more significance was the involvement of Fr Richard Hayes with the anti-Veto agitation in 1815. The British government was willing to grant concessions provided it was allowed a veto in the appointment of bishops. Fr Hayes, a Wexfordman, spent two years in Rome petitioning the Holy See not to concede the power of veto to the government. His mission ended in confusion and Daniel O'Connell eventually paid part of the bill for his expenses.

O'Connell was friendly with the Franciscans. His family kept the head of Fr Francis O'Sullivan ofm, who had been killed while saying mass in 1653, on Scariff Island in Kenmare Bay, as a relic. The head was stolen in 1847, but was mysteriously returned to Derrynane in 1931 and was presented to the friars in Killarney a decade later. In the 1820s O'Connell gave much helpful advice to the friars, especially when they were engaged in re-building some of their churches. His life-long friend, Fr Roger O'Higgins ofm organized the erection of a monument to him in Limerick in 1857.

Catholic Emancipation was politically motivated, and the bill approving it was only passed after certain precautions had been built in by the British parliament. The loss of the franchise by small freeholders was the most significant consequence, but the second half of the Emancipation Bill contained legislation by which the activities of regulars and Jesuits could be severely restricted. All friars in the country were to register, all novitiates were to close, no further friars would be allowed to return from the Continent and so the religious Orders would slowly die out. Only female Orders and diocesan congregations would survive.

This legislation was the equivalent of that which led to the suppression of the Jesuits on the Continent. The passing of the Emancipation Bill in 1829 caused dismay among the friars. They had second thoughts about plans for expansion and re-building. Despite the assurances of Daniel O'Connell that the law could not and would not be enforced, it was a number of years before the friars felt safe again. In fact the law was enforced, but only in a very limited number of cases dealing with charitable bequests and with the payment of rates. Although removed from the English statute-book, it remained in Irish law until the process of removing obsolete legislation began in the 1980s. In this century it was used to impose the payment of domestic rates, especially after a celebrated incident in Athlone in 1916.

55

In response to that situation the Irish Franciscans began to think of foreign missions. Details of the first such venture in Newfoundland will be discussed in Chapter 5, in addition to an account of Irish involvement with the one truly international unit within the Order, the Custody of the Holy Land.

In Ireland the friary churches of this period were still comparatively small, with a high altar and perhaps a side altar dedicated to the Blessed Virgin. They were often not as well kept as they might have been. Confessions were heard at a seat in the sanctuary and early in the century the priest had an alms bag hanging nearby. Very often there was a choir to sing during mass, but few friaries had enough priests for a Solemn High Mass. Monstrances were in use, which implies that some form of exposition of the Blessed Sacrament took place. Devotions to the Stations of the Cross were common. Lay associations such as the Third Order (modern Secular Franciscans) and the Cordbearers of St Francis flourished. Questing from the altar in parish churches brought the friars into contact with a large number of people.

As the century progressed the position of the Franciscans in Ireland was consolidated and the decline in vocations ceased. By 1830 the smaller houses had been closed down. St Isidore's College in Rome was functioning normally. The friars were well liked by the people. There were no real financial worries. However, the level of community life and of regular observance was extremely low and it would be hard to distinguish the way of life of a Franciscan from that of a diocesan priest.

Religious life on the Continent had undergone sweeping changes due to the French Revolution. Whole Franciscan provinces had been wiped out. Numbers dropped from c. seventy-seven thousand in 1762 to fifteen thousand in 1830. 'Regular Observance' – an insistence on the importance of external behaviour as a sign of religious witness – was seen as the key to renewal. The man of external discipline was bound to be a true Christian within. The logical conclusion of this movement on the Continent was the extreme ultramontanism of the late nineteenth and early twentieth centuries of which Cardinal Cullen was the strongest advocate in Ireland.

The concept of regular observance was new to the Irish Franciscans. Since they enjoyed the confidence of people, they saw no reason for changing their way of life. Their history from 1830 to the end of the century is the story of how pressure from the Continent forced them to adopt new practice of regular observance.

## Nineteenth-Century Reform and Re-structuring

Fr Henry Hughes became provincial of the Irish Franciscans in 1837.

There were then sixteen houses in Ireland with about fifty-five priests. Practically all the buildings had been renovated within the preceding ten years and the last closure of a house (Ross) had taken place in 1832. The students were trained in Rome. Capranica had been rented out in order to provide finances for the students. The mission in Newfoundland was prospering under Dr Fleming, while the first Irish Franciscans would soon depart for Australia.

The minister general, Fr Bartholomew Altemir, wrote to Fr Hughes on 3 September 1837, drawing his attention to certain shortcomings. As Fr Hughes passed through the friaries on visitation, he imposed various obligations mentioned in the general's letter: proper care of the churches, attention to saying mass correctly, community meditation, common recitation of the Divine Office, proper libraries and archives, and a need for theological conferences.

Fr Hughes went to Rome in 1839 to discuss problems which had arisen between the friars of Waterford and the local bishop. While there, he was appointed vicar apostolic of Gibraltar, where he became the first non-Spanish bishop. Gibraltar had just been sundered from the diocese of Cadiz and Dr Hughes became a British public hero when he was harassed by the Spanish and by some local Catholics. He resigned in 1845 and retired to Ireland, where he died in 1860.

After Fr Hughes had departed for Gibraltar, the friars reverted to their old ways. The pace of change slackened. Most interest seems to have been focussed on elections at the provincial chapters. In 1839 the minister general ordered that civil province of origin was no longer to be considered a factor in elections at provincial level. While this directive was theoretically obeyed, a deeply ingrained tradition going back for more than two centuries did not die out overnight.

The Great Famine had little direct effect on the friars. The friars responded to the disaster by raising funds to relieve distress. Bishop Hughes for example, sent £100 from Gibraltar. Its social effects may have led to the closure of the friaries in Meelick and Claregalway in 1847-8. In 1850 there was a debate about the custom of eating meat on Saturdays. In the meantime, the national synod had been held at Thurles and a number of conscientious friars were worried about their way of life. One of these, Fr Peter (Francis) O'Farrell, was appointed visitator of the Irish province in 1852.

Fr O'Farrell's first effort was to try to enforce the decrees made by Fr Hughes. In this he used further letters from the minister general and the decisions of the Synod of Thurles. He also added some injunctions of his own, in particular the wearing of the habit both inside and outside the friary. The provincial chapter following the visitation broke up in disarray as Fr O'Farrell, supported by the new archbishop of Dublin, Dr Cullen, tried to force his ideas on the friars. Thereafter the minister general decided to appoint the new superiors of the province. Following further disputes about reform in 1853-4 Fr O'Farrell went to Australia, where he continued to work for 'regular observance'. The friars continued in their former way of life, and Dr Cullen began to think of the reform 'of a certain religious Order' as a priority.

From 1852 until his death in 1878, Dr Cullen played an active role in the life of the religious Orders, using his title of apostolic visitator of the religious of Ireland. He closely vetted those friars who were likely to become provincials. He insisted that the visitator general confer with him during the visitation. He would then decide whether the visitator could hold the provincial chapter, in which case the superiors would be elected, or should hold a provincial congregation, in which case the superiors would be appointed from Rome, often on the recommendation of Dr Cullen himself. The Franciscan authorities in Rome, who also wished to reform the Irish province, but in their own way, quietly resisted his efforts. By 1870 they were able to by-pass him.

In 1857 a Belgian friar, Fr Bernard van Loo, was appointed visitator general and reformer of the Irish province. In the aftermath of the French Revolution, the Belgian Franciscan province had become extinct and was re-established in 1842. The loss of the English Franciscan college at Douai had been followed by the curtailment of religious in England under the provisions of the Catholic Emancipation Act. As a result, the English province had no novitiate, and was reduced to four members by 1850. Contact was established between the remaining English friars and the vigorous new Belgian province through the Franciscan nuns at Taunton in 1848. A decade passed before the Belgians had sufficient priests to make their first foundation in England at Sclerder. After years of steady progress, a full English province was re-erected in 1891.

Fr Bernard van Loo was closely associated with the Belgian mission to England. A native of Ghent, he had been a diocesan priest before joining the Belgian friars in 1844. He came to England in 1849 to negotiate the coming of the Belgian Franciscans and he was insistent that the key to Franciscan life was strict observance of the Rule. At the general chapter at Rome in 1856 – the first full chapter for nearly a hundred years – he was elected procurator general of the Recollects and Alcantarines, and the following year he was sent to Ireland.

Fr van Loo conducted a quick, vigorous and efficient visitation in each friary, and clearly outlined the abuses he encountered. He persuaded the provincial chapter and definitory to accept a special set of statutes for Ireland, based on a summary of general legislation and on the Belgian statutes. The new provincial was not elected, but was very carefully chosen by Rome. He was Fr L. Cosgrove, and was picked for his personal dedication to reform. Within a few years he had arranged for the opening of a strict novitiate at Drogheda, and promulgated new regulations for the students in Rome. He further rationalized the number of friaries in Ireland with the aim of concentrating the remaining friars in larger communities where they could lead a common life. No further effort was made to re-open Meelick. The community in Claregalway was withdrawn to Galway – but they continued to say mass on Sundays in the old church for a number of years. Youghal friary at Aglish was closed in 1862 and it took the personal intervention of the archbishop of Cashel to keep Thurles open (1860).

Fr van Loo had used his visit to Ireland to make arrangements for the first new house of the Belgians in England. Before leaving Ireland, he also decided that the Belgian Franciscans would open a house at Gorey. He hoped that the process of reform in Ireland would be encouraged by the good example of the new Belgian community. The first friars arrived at Gorey in October 1858. They acted as chaplains to the Ram family and to the Franciscan Sisters of Perpetual Adoration. It proved impossible to turn Gorey into an ideal Franciscan house. On the invitation of the bishop, Dr Moriarty, the friars moved to Killarney in July 1860. The new friary there became the novitiate of the English province. One of the Irishmen who joined the English friars through Killarney was Fr David Fleming. He became a noted theologian, deeply involved in the theological controversies of his times. He was a member of the various commissions on Anglican Orders, of the Biblical Commission and of other papal bodies in Rome. He became the first provincial of the newly erected English province in 1891 and governed the whole Order as vicar general in 1901-3. He played a significant part in the handing over of Killarney to the Irish friars in 1902.

After Fr van Loo left Ireland, he remained in contact with the situation and used his influence in Rome to keep up pressure for reform. A succession of visitators repeated the same points time and time again: divine office in choir, annual retreats, monthly recollection, theological conferences, Stations of the Cross, the giving of missions and retreats. Propaganda Fide became more closely involved with the situation in Ireland. The use of titular guardianates, as a result of which practically every priest in the province was entitled to attend the provincial chapter, ceased in 1873 by order of the minister general, backed by Propaganda. The chapter of 1870 became known as the Magnum Capitulum (Great Chapter) since it was the last time all the titular guardians attended. The minister general of the Order, Bernardine dal Vago, visited Ireland in person in the autumn of 1872, the first time the general had come since the end of the thirteenth century! Fr dal Vago laid great stress on the need for a common life in the Irish friaries and he hoped that newly ordained priests would be stationed in houses where the level of religious observance was high.

The Irish Franciscans did not see the need for many of these changes. The friars saw themselves as having survived two centuries of persecution. They were liked by the people and pastorally effective. While most communities were small, they normally had two public masses on weekdays – an early one for workers (7 or 8 a.m.) and a later one for the general public (10 or 11 a.m.). But neither the Eucharistic fast nor the practice of the people favoured frequent Communion. Rosary and benediction, occasionally with a sermon, took place on many evenings. Confessions were heard after daily masses, on Friday nights and on Saturday morning and evening. Stations of the cross were held in public on Friday nights. A perpetual novena to the Blessed Virgin (and often to St Anthony as well) took place each week, and from eight to ten tridua or novenae were held during the course of the year. With so much religious activity and with reasonably full congregations, the Irish friars did not take kindly to talk of further reform.

Once again new statutes for the Irish province were passed at the provincial chapter in 1873. Everybody, including the authorities in Rome, agreed that they were excellent. All that was missing was the will to implement them. However, the visitors continued to press for reform and even found a new abuse which they wished to stamp out – the presence of female cooks and housekeepers in the friaries. The friars maintained that the situation was satisfactory. They were not unduly worried about the decline in vocations, as the province had remained the same size (sixty priests) for most of the decade. They were looking back to a glorious past rather than forward to future challenges – the classic symptom of an organization in decline. There was little zeal for innovation or adaptation, and the impetus for reform would come, once again, from outside.

*Decorative carving, Inchiquin tomb, Ennis Friary, Co. Clare*

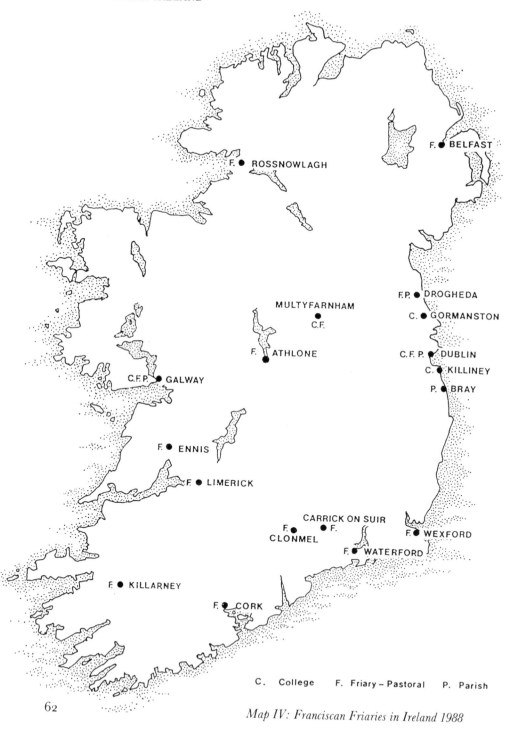

F. ● BELFAST

F. ● ROSSNOWLAGH

MULTYFARNHAM
● 
C.F.

F.P. ● DROGHEDA

C. ● GORMANSTON

F. ● ATHLONE

C.F.P. ● DUBLIN

C. ● KILLINEY

P. ● BRAY

C.F.P. ● GALWAY

F. ● ENNIS

F. ● LIMERICK

CARRICK ON SUIR
F. ● 
F. ● 
CLONMEL

F. ● WEXFORD

F. ● WATERFORD

F. ● KILLARNEY

F. ● CORK

C.  College    F.  Friary – Pastoral    P.  Parish

*Map IV: Franciscan Friaries in Ireland 1988*

# Chapter 4

# VATICAN I TO VATICAN II
## (1870-1988)

The Council of Trent had inspired the last great renewal of Irish Franciscanism in the seventeenth century. Much of the inspiration underlying the renewal which took place in the late nineteenth and early twentieth centuries came from the first Vatican Council held in 1869-70. The spirit of the Counter-Reformation had been primarily aggressive. That of Vatican I was primarily defensive. According to Roger Aubert the Council stressed, 'precise doctrine on papal authority . . . a more authoritive and centralized Church structure . . . a new piety, which insisted more on reception of the sacraments and multiplicity of external practices than on interior piety'. This is understandable given the attacks on the Church, both physical and intellectual, which had occurred during the nineteenth century. The French Revolution and the Revolutions of 1848 had contained strong anti-clerical elements. Church property was seized and laws restricting the Church's political and social role were passed. Parallel to these attacks on the institutional Church, many of the intellectual movements of the century such as Darwinism and Marxism questioned fundamental tenets of the Church's teaching and led to a growing sense of doubt.

Though most of these movements had little direct impact on Ireland, their effects were felt indirectly through the general retrenchment taking place in the European Church. In particular, the Irish Franciscans underwent considerable organizational changes in the late nineteenth century. The existing complement of friars, called 'Black friars' because they dressed as clergymen, were gradually replaced by habit-wearing 'Brown friars' who were trained under German control, inward-looking, aware of their sinful condition and living a monastic life. Their attitude is summed up in the words of one of them, 'The devil is waiting to grab you once you leave the door of your friary.' The older and more traditional friars felt a sense of injustice at the treatment being given to them and strongly resisted the attempts to phase them out. However, the new spirit triumphed and ushered in a period of intensive activity and high achievement by Irish Franciscans.

63

## Late Nineteenth-Century German Influence

Like the Belgian province, the German provinces were badly affected by the French Revolution. The province of Saxony managed to survive, though it had come very close to dying out. After 1850 it was rebuilt and expanded under Fr Gregor Janknecht, provincial in 1855-61, 1867-79 and again in 1888-91, and definitor general in 1862-7. He sent the first group of German friars to the USA, where they founded the Sacred Heart province. Fr Janknecht was twice appointed visitator general of the Irish province, in 1879 and in 1888. Both visits were highly significant. He was initially quite impressed by the level of reform which had been achieved in Ireland, but gradually came to realize that more radical reform was needed. He became convinced that the Irish were beyond reform. They talked and passed resolutions but were incapable of effective action. They would never reform themselves. Reform would have to be imposed on them from outside: 'the tree uprooted and replanted'.

This was the era of the *Kulturkampf* – the conflict of authority between the newly established German state and the Catholic Church – during which Franciscan life in Germany was severely restricted and a number of students fled to the USA to finish their studies. One of these was Joseph (Bernard) Doebbing. Son of a Münster cobbler, he had joined the friars in 1873 at the age of eighteen. Following his ordination, he pursued higher studies and was transferred to the Franciscan House of Studies at Quaracchi, near Florence, in 1881. There he met Fr Luke Carey, guardian of St Isidore's College, probably through Fr Janknecht. Fr Carey was a keen reformer and was looking for lectors to train students at St Isidore's. The Irish did not train their own teachers and depended on other provinces, especially the Italians. He was impressed by Fr Doebbing and invited him to Rome to promote reform among the young Irish friars. The minister general approved the proposal, seeing it as the first step towards the reform of the whole Irish province.

Fr Doebbing was appointed lector at St Isidore's on 10 October 1883. He became master of students on 5 December. As an experiment he sent some students to the College of Propaganda Fide, but they found the course there too difficult. A group of German brothers arrived to look after the needs of the community at St Isidore's. They were soon followed by a group of German students and lectors, so that the Irish clerics could be taught regular life by example and given lectures in theology within the college. Some financial aid was also sent from Germany to help in the upkeep. The more turbulent Irish students were sent to spend some time in smaller Italian friaries.

At the suggestion of the minister general, who was encouraged by

Fr Janknecht, the Irish provincial chapter of 1885 agreed to send the Irish postulants to do their novitiate under German control, mainly at the new novitiate of the Saxony province at Harreveld in Holland.

When Fr Janknecht returned to Ireland as visitor in 1888 he still had to make a final decision about reform. He carried with him a decree sanctioning total reform of the Irish province which had already been signed by the minister general but which he was not authorized to publish. By the time of the provincial chapter he had made up his mind, contacted Rome, and been instructed to proclaim the document. The consent of Propaganda Fide had been obtained by the minister general for the plan. No novices could be received in Ireland for six years. Fr Doebbing was appointed delegate general for St Isidore's, where the rights of the Irish province would be suspended for the time being, (this appointment was later extended to cover Capranica and the new foundation of St Elia). Newly ordained priests would remain on the Continent until there was a sufficient number to take over two houses in Ireland, one of which would then become the novitiate. Formation would be totally reorganized through a seraphic college, a novitiate and a house for the study of humanities and philosophy in Ireland, with theology remaining in Rome where Brothers would also receive a proper training. (The seraphic college was initially in Capranica, later transferred to Multyfarnham; the novitiate was set up at Ennis and after a short time moved to Killarney, where the clerics originally studied humanities and philosophy; later they went to University Colleges Cork or Galway; on the Continent philosophy and theoretical courses were based at Louvain and Rome respectively.) The older friars would be allowed to continue in their traditional life and would be replaced by reformed friars on a house by house basis.

The Irish provincial, Fr Jackman, went to Rome to appeal to Propaganda Fide, apparently in ignorance of the procedures which had been followed. He pointed to the considerable progress towards a complete reform which had been made by the older friars. At the general congregation of Propaganda Fide on 1 April 1889, the cardinals unanimously backed the action of the minister general. There could be no further appeal.

The minister general was satisfied with the outcome. He recalled the success of the Belgian-English house in Killarney and praised the old friars for their efforts at reform. In particular he was grateful that all housekeepers and female cooks had gone from the friaries. He was sure that the friars would be happy with the complete reform which was now to be imposed.

Fr Janknecht was pleased that the revitalized province of Saxony had been healthy enough to cure an ailing sister province. Following his success in introducing reform to St Isidore's, Fr Doebbing resigned in 1898, became involved in affairs at the Franciscan curia and was nominated bishop of Nepi and Sutri on 1 April 1900. Being a German bishop in an Italian diocese, he was in a difficult position during the First World War. He died on 14 March 1916, having been a capable administrator of his diocese for sixteen years.

Though happy that his efforts to improve standards of theology at St Isidore's had succeeded, Fr Carey was annoyed at the treatment of the Irish province and left the college. A bitter row broke out when he was falsely accused of maladministration and this soured his later years. He returned to St Isidore's after Irish control was restored and died there in 1924.

Fr Jackman, the provincial, and most of the older friars resented the way the reform had been pushed through. They petitioned various Irish organizations and newspapers, including several local government bodies, but to no avail. They had understood 'a reform of the novitiate' to mean building a new novitiate in Ennis, and not to mean training the novices in a new spirit. Most of them were happy to be let live out their days in peace. A number joined the new reformers when they arrived in Ireland. Some did leave the province, or the Order, to work as priests elsewhere. From 1890 on, the old friars concentrated their efforts on making sure that the Germans would not retain St Isidore's and Capranica. They did not mind the Germans retaining the new foundation at St Elia.

The last non-reform Irish provincial chapter met in 1895. The first group of reformers, Frs Peter Begley and Nicholas Dillon, with two other priests and two brothers, returned to Ireland in 1896. Despite a last stand by the old friars, which finally ended after mediation efforts by Bishop Thomas Nulty of Meath, the new friars were able to take over Multyfarnham as the first house of the reform on 11 December 1896.

1897 was an important year for the Franciscan Order, since in that year Leo XIII promulgated a uniform set of general constitutions for the whole Order, doing away with the distinctions between Observant and Reformed, Discalced and Recollect.

A provincial chapter was due in 1899, but permission to hold it was refused. The general definitorium, by virtue of a rescript of Propaganda Fide, appointed a new provincial administration: Fr Peter Begley as provincial, Fr Bernard Cooney, a supporter of the 'old' friars, as custos, and four definitors. The minister general laid down the basic rules in his letter promulgating the appointments: the general constitutions were to be observed; certain houses were to be given to the new friars; those who wished to continue in the old way of life were to be assigned to special convents. At this time only

Multyfarnham and Ennis had been taken over, soon to be followed by Athlone, while Cork had been designated as the friary where the old friars who wished to live a strict life could stay. The date of this decree, 2 March 1899, may be taken as the day when the Irish province adopted a new expression of Franciscanism.

As the Brown Franciscans gradually took over the friaries in Ireland they discovered the good-will which the people had towards the Black friars. Many of these old friars became prominent figures in the folklore of friary towns. For example Fr Mick or Fr Mack (Fr James Theodosius McNamara died 1881) in Thurles, and Fr Thomas (Joseph) Rossiter, who died in 1928, in Carrick-on-Suir. At the end of the nineteenth century there were about one hundred and ten friars in the province and about seven novices joined each year. A further ten friars worked on the Australian mission, where the first local vocations were beginning to emerge. There were thirteen friaries in Ireland (Thurles had been closed in 1892, and Killarney handed over to the Irish in 1902), two on the Continent and three in Australia. The majority of the friars were Munstermen, mainly from Clare and Limerick.

The new Brown friars were typical of the Catholic Church in the era following the Vatican I. The stress was on centralized government, which produced a series of rules and regulations governing every aspect of a friar's life. Formal devotions were introduced and drew large congregations. As more young priests and brothers came back from the Continent, the friaries in Ireland were taken over one by one, Cork in 1910, Wexford and Galway in 1918, Dublin after the death of Archbishop Walsh in 1921, Drogheda in 1923 and Carrick-on-Suir the following year, finally Waterford in 1927.

The reform ran into some problems. A number of the Black friars opted to become diocesan priests or military chaplains. The reformers fell out among themselves, especially over the support given to Fr Luke Carey by Fr Benignus Gannon, who was provincial in 1903-5 and 1908-11. The attitude of Fr John Capistran Hanrahan who was elected minister provincial in 1911, was considered unsound and he was replaced by Fr Nicholas Dillon in 1912. Fr John was appointed the next provincial in 1918 and supervised the implementation of some of the final regulations of the reform, such as those concerning the wearing of the habit. The opening of St Anthony's Hall in Cork in 1909 enabled the young Franciscan students to attend UCC, but the experiment was premature and the Hall was closed after a couple of years. While the reform movement seemed dour and cold at first, the Brown friars soon adapted to Irish conditions and many of them emerged as 'characters' in their own right.

67

*St Francis, Ennis Friary, Co. Clare*

0          15 cm

## Development and Expansion of the Province

As with most other Orders, vocations to the Irish Franciscans rose rapidly after the First World War. The number of friars increased from one hundred and ten in 1900, to one hundred and fifty by 1920, to two hundred and twenty-five in 1930 and to two hundred and fifty in 1945. By 1960 the total had reached four hundred, eventually peaking at four hundred and thirty in 1965. This represented a return to the high figures of the early 1700s. Numbers have since declined to around two hundred and fifty. One reason is that the missions in South Africa and Central America have become independent. The number of vocations in Ireland has also dropped. In the period 1970-86 about ten entered the novitiate each year but only four persevered. Whereas in the period 1950-9 eighteen entered each year and nine persevered. A further reason for the decline in numbers is that the novitiate was closed in 1987 pending a reorganization of the formation course.

The Irish friars were not greatly involved in the turbulent events of 1914-18. A few friars served as chaplains to armies in various parts of the world. For instance Fr Leo Sheehan entered Jerusalem with the Camel Corps under General Allenby in December 1917, while Fr Isidore O'Meehan was accidentally shot in Iraq in 1919. Similarly the events of 1916-21 in Ireland had little direct impact on the friars. A hall at Merchant's Quay, Dublin, was used for IRA training before 1916. Individual friars were involved in the Republican movement on a personal basis. Perhaps the most famous of these was the young Fr Philip Murphy. His intense interest in social problems and his work in labour relations led to his appointment as chaplain to the mayors of Limerick. In this capacity he was deeply involved in the 'Murdered Mayors' incident in 1921, and was forced to leave the city following police raids on the friary. After outstanding work in other parts of Ireland, he went to Australia in 1933, where he died in 1954.

The increase in vocations after 1920 enabled the friars to extend their apostolates. Initially student houses were reorganized. The old college of St Anthony at Louvain in Belgium was bought back by the friars after a gap of a century and re-opened in 1926 as a house of philosophy and theology. St Anthony's College, Galway, opened in 1932. As a result many friars were able to take degree courses at UCG. The Galway college became really important during the Second World War, when Louvain had to be evacuated and communication with Rome became extremely difficult. The re-opening of the college in Louvain was symptomatic of another interest of the friars of the 1920s – an awareness of the history of the Irish Franciscans, and especially their important contribution to life, religion and politics in seventeenth-century Ireland. Thus the new friary church at Athlone was built to honour the Four Masters. Later the new friary at Rossnowlagh was seen as the re-incarnation of Donegal friary, while a special institute for research into Irish Franciscan history and Irish culture was founded at Killiney in 1945.

One reason for the stress on third-level education was a reaction to the situation in the previous century when the Irish had been unable to provide their own lecturers. Since 1930 practically all ordained

Irish Franciscans have had two if not three university degrees. Many friars have done doctorates, mainly in the ecclesiastical sciences and several have become university professors, particularly in UCG, but also in UCD, QUB, NUU (Coleraine) and several pontifical universities in Rome. Among the better known were Fr Felim O'Briain in UCG for his contribution to sociology in the 1950s, Fr Colmán Ó Huallacháin for his work on the Irish language, and Fr Alexander Kerrigan for his studies on scripture, especially his contribution to the Vatican II. The work of the Institute in Killiney in Irish literature (Fr Padraig Ó Suilleabháin) and history (Fr Canice Mooney) has won considerable recognition, and *Collectanea Hibernica*, the periodical devoted to Irish historical sources, published from there, is well-known to scholars. There have even been a few Irish Franciscan novelists (Frs Thomas Fitzgerald and Sebastian Lee) and poets (Fr Lucius McClean).

The Irish friars also became involved in popular religious publications. Magazines included the *Irish Franciscan Tertiary* (1891-9 and 1911-14), *Irish Franciscan Almanac* (1926-31), *Assisi* (1929-67), *The Franciscan* (1975-87) and *The Brief* (1946-). Many friars contributed to these and other magazines as well as publishing booklets. Fr Kevin O'Sullivan's commentaries on the Sunday readings and on the Sunday lectionary proved extremely popular with preachers. Several friaries, in particular Dublin, ran 'good reading' crusades with lending libraries in the 1930s.

Education became an important apostolate. The friars had several short-lived secondary schools in the nineteenth century, such as St Francis's Academy in Clonmel (1873-81) and St Bonaventure's Academy in Athlone (1871-8). The reformers singled out lack of proper second-level education as one of the problems of the province. A seraphic college for young boys thinking of entering the Order opened in Capranica, north of Rome, in 1891. Because of its distance from Ireland it never had more than a dozen pupils each year. The college was transferred to Multyfarnham in 1899 and eventually expanded to take one hundred and fifteen pupils. As early as 1924 doubts were expressed about the suitability of Multyfarnham as a site for a major college. Land at Gormanston was purchased in 1947 and the first pupils of the new open college arrived there in 1954. Multyfarnham then became an agricultural college. A new building for that purpose was opened in 1982 to accommodate up to one hundred and twenty students. In the mid-1960s the friars began teaching religion at the request of the archbishop of Dublin. Quite a number have worked in this capacity in Bolton Street, as well as in a supervisory capacity within the archdiocese and in other schools, technical, vocational, community and secondary, in Ireland.

The Brown friars took over a well-run system of pastoral churches. The increase of vocations in the 1930s caused concern that there would not be sufficient accommodation for all the friars. One response was the opening of foreign missions, initially in China, later in Africa. Education and studies absorbed more, but the majority of new priests found their way into pastoral friaries. While only a few houses were enlarged as a result (Dublin, Clonmel, Cork) many of the churches were re-built or extended (Athlone, Carrick-on-Suir, Cork, Drogheda, Dublin, Limerick and Waterford) and a new friary was founded at Rossnowlagh in 1946. In the spirit of Vatican I, great stress was laid on the externals. Masses, benedictions and devotions were increased although those to St Paschal Baylon, patron of Eucharistic devotions, never became popular. While the number of novenae and tridua were reduced slightly, more emphasis was placed on those retained, especially to the Immaculate Conception and to St Anthony. More priests meant more confession boxes and extended hours for hearing. A movement begun by Fr Francis Donnelly and later taken up by Fr Philip Murphy led to many people dedicating their houses to the Name of Jesus by placing little blue plaques with the initials IHS over the door. More friars became involved in giving parish missions and retreats, and a special handbook was prepared for this purpose. In some places the friars helped the parish clergy by doing supply. But some of the clergy saw the friars as a threat and tried to restrict the work they were allowed to do.

The Franciscan Third Order (now the Order of Secular Franciscans) had existed in Ireland for centuries. There are references as early as 1270 to people seeking burial in the Franciscan habit, an indication that they were tertiaries. In 1470 a lady was given honorary membership of the Order. There are few references to tertiaries during the period of persecution under Elizabeth I but early in the seventeenth century it was again active – shown by the publication of a handbook in Irish at Louvain in 1641. After another period in obscurity during the Penal period, the Third Order re-emerged as a flourishing organization in Dublin under Fr Francis Fleming after 1759. The next period of vitality began in the 1920s. Much of the literary activity already noted was connected with the Third Order, especially the magazines and lending libraries. So many joined that it became necessary to divide them into male and female sections. Members became involved in social work, for example getting plots for market gardening for the poor in Athlone in the 1930s. Going on pilgrimages became a form of devotion for tertiaries between the wars. In 1926 ten trains brought pilgrims to Athlone for the Franciscan year celebrations. Local groups went to such places as the friary ruins at Askeaton, Claregalway and Muckross, while a major national Third Order pilgrimage assembled at Cashel in 1929. Knock was a site of Franciscan pilgrimages from its early days as a shrine and these increased greatly in the 1930s – five thousand travelled from Limerick in 1937. The Franciscan Sunday in Knock is still one of the biggest of the year. The first national Franciscan pilgrimage to Lourdes took place in 1929 and the second in 1934, after which it became an annual event. The SS *Laurentic* was chartered in 1935. After the Second World War the pilgrimage was resumed, this time by air.

There were a number of events to commemorate special occasions. In 1924 there was a pilgrimage to Athlone to celebrate the seventh centenary of the foundation of Athlone friary and the stigmata of St Francis. In 1926 the Franciscan year to commemorate the seventh centenary of St Francis' death was held and marked by pilgrimages to Athlone and to Italy. The Irish travellers to the Continent also attended the opening of the new St Anthony's College in Louvain. The tercentenary of the death of Br Micheál Ó Cléirigh was celebrated in 1944. There was a pilgrimage to Rome for the Holy Year in 1950, and the tercentenary of the death of Fr Luke Wadding was commemorated in the Wadding Year, 1956-7.

In addition to its very obvious presence in a town a friary also serves an extensive hinterland. Thus the friary in Athlone serves people in western Westmeath, northern Offaly, eastern and central Galway, south Roscommon and south Longford. In this regard the friars are the direct descendants of the old Irish monks as the spiritual advisers to the ordinary faithful. People often seek a particular item from the friars: blessed salt in the midlands, holy water in Munster. Special powers are often associated with an individual friar, for example Fr Columba Hanrahan in Athlone, Fr X-avier Power [*sic*] in Multyfarnham, or Br Paschal Burke in Drogheda.

Professed brothers were re-introduced into the Irish province by the Brown friars. There had been brothers previously – Micheál Ó Cléirigh was a brother – but the tradition had died out by the nineteenth century. The place of the brother was taken by the perpetual tertiary. During the reform under Fr Doebbing, a number of Irish lay-novices were given special training both in the spiritual life and in trades by German brothers. Brothers have continued in this lifestyle since.

## Vatican II and After

In 1960, as they were preparing to celebrate the Patrician Year, the Irish Franciscans were still imbued with the spirit of Vatican I. Fr Celsus O'Brien was elected minister provincial at the chapter in 1960 and remained in charge until 1972. His twelve years in office coincide with the period of change associated with Vatican II. By 1972 the surface changes associated with the Ecumenical Council had taken place and a deeper appreciation of what these implied was beginning to emerge.

The initial Irish Franciscan reaction to Pope John's Council was excitement, and a desire to follow the lead from Rome. Two members of the Irish province were periti. The first changes were taken up with enthusiasm, especially those relating to the liturgy, such as changing around sanctuaries for mass facing the people, and saying mass in the vernacular. Some friars became involved in youth work, in discussion groups and in lectures on the spirit of the Council.

It was necessary to update legislation within the Order. New General Constitutions were issued in 1967, again in 1973 and, after the new Code of Canon Law had appeared, in 1987. Each change obliged the Irish friars to update their own statutes. Commissions were set up to study various areas and an extraordinary provincial chapter was held in 1968. Several commissions followed as each succeeding provincial chapter updated legislation. Such legal work was useful and necessary but it betrayed the negative attitudes of Vatican I: laws were there to limit rather than to encourage.

Changes introduced by the general constitutions affected the life of the friars. The old division between brothers and clerics vanished. Brothers were encouraged to move into new occupations. In 1968 many availed of the option of dropping the religious name. Communities came to have a much greater say in what was happening in their own houses. While friars answered the call of Pope John XXIII for priests in Latin America, moves were initiated to make the missions in South Africa, and eventually those in Central America as well, independent. Dialogue was encouraged between superiors and subjects. The use of money by friars was permitted – previously it had been held by lay people in the name of the friars.

The period since Vatican II has brought changes in apostolates. The move into religious education has already been noted. Previously friars had been involved as chaplains to CIE and to the hotels in Dublin. Several friars became chaplains to other organizations. Bishops offered parishes to friars, beginning with Wood Quay in Galway in 1971. The positive aspect of this was a genuine desire to involve the friars in diocesan life, but there was also an element of giving them problem parishes where few people lived in city-centre areas, or where there was a shortage of priests. Friary doors opened and more people were welcomed inside. Confession bells were introduced to make the sacrament more readily available. Questing was seen as a form of pastoral visitation putting more people in contact with priests. Updating of the Secular Franciscan Order became a

73

priority, with less stress on monthly meetings and more on personal spiritual progress. Efforts were made to make the liturgy correspond more with people's needs, through the introduction of folk groups, for example.

Despite all these changes a sense of purpose was lacking. Young men were joining the province but not many were staying. The departure of priests to get married, while not seen as a problem for those remaining, indicated some form of malaise. Democratization was welcomed but produced an inability to make decisions. Thus St Anthony's College, Louvain, which had become surplus to requirements due to linguistic changes in Belgium in 1967, was kept open pending a decision for a decade and a half. Then in 1983 it was decided to re-open it as the Irish Institute for European Affairs run entirely by lay staff. But a small house was built so that the friars could continue to live there!

It is difficult to pinpoint the origins of an awareness that a vision of life was missing. A number of friars carried out experiments with a hermitage style house-of-prayer. Others did long renewal courses, either the 'Focus for Action' course for religious or that organized by the NCPI for priests. Significantly the provincial chapter of 1981, in addition to renewing statutes, set a number of goals for the friars. The same happened in 1984. A realization was growing that Vatican II, like Vatican I and Trent, was about a way of Christian living rather than just a legislative body. At all levels of life within the Order shackles were being shaken off.

The provincial chapter of 1987 decided to enter into a process of renewal and review of ministries, the initial phase of which would last over a year. Its theme is based on the words of St Francis: 'Let us begin, brothers, to serve the Lord God, for up to now we have made little or no progress.'

*Original seal of the Franciscan Order in Ireland c. 1530*

# Chapter 5

# FOREIGN MISSIONS

When the followers of St Francis first came to Ireland it was on the edge of the Christian world. As the great colonial powers began to expand in the sixteenth century the Tudor monarchs treated Ireland as one of their colonies. Thus the Irish Franciscans had little opportunity to participate in the missionary movements of those years. There was a short rescue mission to Scotland early in the seventeenth century. Individual friars worked in many parts of the world in the eighteenth and nineteenth centuries. But the first organized mission was that to Newfoundland which began in 1784. During the nineteenth and twentieth centuries the Irish Franciscans undertook missionary work in many parts of the world, including Australia, China, South Africa and Latin America.

Since the time when Friar James of Ireland is reputed to have accompanied Blessed Odoric of Pordenone to China in 1316-20, Irish Franciscans have worked best as individuals. They have been less successful in organized missionary activity. In Scotland, Newfoundland and Australia they were initially problem-solvers rather than planners. They were effective in implanting the Church but not the Order. As a result Newfoundland was left without a Franciscan presence and the same would have happened in Australia but for the vision of one friar. The missionaries in South Africa and Zimbabwe were slow to set up a formation system for young Franciscans but the Order is now flourishing in both countries.

## The Holy Land

The custody of the Holy Land is the only truly international unit within the Franciscan Order. St Francis went there to see for himself and experience the places where Christ had lived among men. His followers set up a friary in Jerusalem between 1222 and 1230. Over the centuries they have become the official custodians of the shrines belonging to the Latin Church. The first Irish Franciscans in the Holy Land were Simon Fitzsimons and Hugh the Illuminator, who left Ireland in 1322. Hugh died in Cairo, but it seems likely Simon returned to Europe since a manuscript account of their journey exists. An Irishman, James Brassel, was superior in Aleppo 1647-9 but belonged to a Spanish province of the Order. Frs Bonaventure Burke, Anthony Mulvey and Bonaventure Kensly worked at the basilica of the Holy Sepulchre, in Sidon and in Aleppo in the last quarter of the seventeenth century. Similarly in the following century Irish Franciscans worked in Bethlehem, Damascus, Jerusalem and on the island of Cyprus.

Fr Bonaventure McLoughlin went to work in Alexandria in 1840 but the climate affected his health. Two Irish friars were in the Holy Land in the 1860s: Frs Aloysius Stafford (Holy Sepulchre, 1861-8) and James Anthony Mahoney (Cairo and Suez, 1862-6). Fr Aloysius was well-known for looking after English-speaking visitors to Jerusalem until he got a stroke and was invalided back to Ireland, where he died in 1882. Fr James had to contend with an outbreak of cholera and returned to Rome a near-broken man. Fr Augustine Holohan was the first of a series of military chaplains when he took up work in Cyprus in 1884. Towards the end of the century two friars produced accounts of the mission in the Holy Land. Fr Anthony Slattery's *Palestine: The Mission and the Missionaries*, while Fr Leonard Dunne's remained unpublished due to his death.

The tradition of individual friars working for the Order in the Holy Land has continued in the twentieth century, beginning with Fr Lawrence O'Neill. The best known was Fr Eugene Hoade who worked there from 1929 to 1956 mainly in the Garden of Gethsemane and as chaplain to the Palestine police. His *Guide to the Holy Land* is still popular and has gone through many editions. Other friars who worked there included Fr Francis Hand, Fr P. J. Giblin and Br Conrad McEvoy.

### The Mission to Scotland

As the morale of the Franciscans in Ireland improved in the early seventeenth century, they were able to help their Celtic brethren in Scotland. Fr John Ogilvie, a Scottish friar not to be confused with his Jesuit name-sake, had been living in the new college at Louvain, and returned to Scotland in 1612. The next year he was joined by a Scottish brother, John Stuart, who had the vital local knowledge and who knew Scots Gaelic. Since the Protestant ministers could not speak Gaelic, many of the people were still Catholic but had not seen a priest for nearly fifty years. Br John travelled back and forth to Louvain, where he died in 1625. He supplied fresh information about the mission and encouraged more priests to go there. Financial problems delayed the departure of Frs Patrick Brady for the Highlands and Edmund McCann for the Hebrides until 4 January 1619. Fr Edmund was arrested and banished. He returned with the next group of priests: Frs Paul O'Neill, Patrick Hegarty and Cornelius Ward. The abandoned Third Order friary at Bonamargy in north Antrim was taken over as a base. Lack of funds and the political situation forced the closure of the mission in 1637. Fr Patrick

Hegarty remained at Bonamargy until his death in 1647. Many people sailed across the North Channel to avail of his spiritual services. Four missionaries were selected to re-open the mission, but they could not travel. Efforts to re-open the mission in 1647-8 also failed, but the friars did return before the end of the century. Then in 1667 two brothers, Mark and Francis McDonnell, recently ordained at St Isidore's College in Rome, volunteered for work in the Highlands. After a difficult journey, including shipwreck and being forced to beg their way overland to Newcastle, they began their pastoral work among the Gaelic-speakers of the Highlands early in 1668. Both suffered from ill-health and Fr Mark died late in 1671. Fr Francis was then working on the island of Uist. Poor health forced him to retire to Ireland in 1679. In 1703 it was reported that there were five Irish Franciscans working in Scotland. The last friar there was Fr Anthony Kelly who was recalled to Ireland by his provincial in the 1730s.

## Mission to Newfoundland

A result of the hope which the Irish Franciscans felt during the 1780s was the opening of their first foreign mission – to Newfoundland. In 1763 almost a third of the population there were Irish-speaking Catholics, suffering from neglect and semi-official persecution. Even though some French Franciscans were working there, the Irish often travelled all the way back to Ireland to receive the sacraments. In January 1784 three Waterford-men applied to London for a permanent priest to minister to them in Newfoundland. The British Government approved their request. Later that year an Irish Franciscan, Fr James Louis O'Donnell, arrived as prefect apostolic. A native of Knocklofty, Co. Tipperary, he had studied in Rome and Prague before his ordination in 1770. Fr O'Donnell was minister provincial in 1779-82. After his arrival in Newfoundland, other friars came to help him. The prefecture became a vicariate on 5 January 1796 and Fr O'Donnell was consecrated bishop at Quebec on 2 September 1796. He resigned in 1807 and returned to Ireland, where he died in 1811.

By 1800 the population of Newfoundland was 35,000 of whom 27,000 (75 per cent) were Catholics. The island was divided into four regions for pastoral purposes but there were only six priests. Both the fish barons and the authorities made life difficult for Catholics. In 1790 a site for a church was refused because it might encourage the Irish to stay overnight. The government was also slow in paying a promised allowance of £75 p.a. The French Revolution caused further difficulties such as looking after the spiritual needs of French prisoners-of-war, or having the holy oils captured by a French frigate 77 in 1794. While on visitation in 1794, the bishop's ship was blown out to sea and drifted among icebergs for three days. His successor broke his ribs while climbing over a fallen tree on a visitation in 1808.

Bishop O'Donnell's successor was Dr Patrick Lambert, who had been Irish Franciscan provincial in 1803-4, and coadjutor since 1806. He resigned in 1817. His place was taken by his nephew, Dr Thomas Scallan, who had gone to Newfoundland in 1812. On his death in 1830, he was succeeded by Dr Michael Anthony Fleming, who had come to Newfoundland as a missionary in 1823. An energetic friar, Dr Fleming began to seek new missionaries in Ireland, among both his own Franciscans and the diocesan clergy. By 1837 he could report that there were ten districts with ten good churches and twenty-two others, looked after by seventeen priests and containing thirty-two Catholic schools. In 1841 he laid the foundation stone of the cathedral and became the first bishop of St John's when the vicariate was erected into a diocese in 1847. He also sent the first priest to work in Labrador. He was granted a coadjutor bishop in 1847 and later retired to a residence where he hoped to house a Franciscan community. The new cathedral was finished in time for him to say the first mass there some months before his death in 1850. By then the anti-Catholic phase in Newfoundland's history was over.

Bishop Thomas Mullock, the coadjutor, succeeded Fleming. A Limerickman who studied in Spain, he had already proved himself a capable administrator before his appointment to Newfoundland. Since the episcopate of Bishop O'Donnell the ecclesiastical region of Newfoundland had included Labrador and Greenland. In a series of moves Bishop Mullock persuaded Propaganda Fide to split up this vast area by creating a second diocese in Newfoundland (Harbour Grace, 1856) and joining most of Labrador and Greenland in one unit (Prefecture Apostolic of the North Pole, 1855). In 1855 he could report that about 50,000 of Newfoundland's population of 70,000 were Catholics, looked after by thirty priests. A local seminary was functioning and he hoped that this would meet the need for future diocesan clergy. Before his death in 1869 Bishop Mullock had made it clear that he considered the time had arrived when the Irish Franciscans would no longer be needed in Newfoundland. His successor was the president of Clonliffe College in Dublin, Canon Thomas Power. Circumstances in Ireland had never permitted more than a handful of Irish friars to go as missionaries – between two and five at any given time. The new local seminary led to a growth in local clergy. Irish Franciscan connections with Newfoundland ceased, for all practical purposes, in 1877, when Fr P. A. Slattery, having previously resigned as president of the local seminary, returned to Europe.

78 Another Irish friar volunteered to go to Newfoundland, but was not

sent. Fr Slattery was proposed as bishop of Harbour Grace in 1880, but not appointed. A hundred years of Irish Franciscan work in Newfoundland had ended.

## United States of America

Michael Egan from Limerick was one of the Franciscans appointed by Rome to settle the affairs of St Isidore's College which had gone bankrupt in 1782. In 1803 he left Ireland for the United States and became pastor of St Mary's, Philadelphia. He then applied to Rome that an independent province of the Order should be erected in the USA. This was agreed in 1804 and he was appointed head of the new entity. In the event nothing happened, probably because of the small number of friars in the north-east of the USA and across the border in Canada. At that time another Irish Franciscan, Fr Patrick Lonergan, was working at Waynesburg, south of Pittsburg, having come there from Sportsman's Hall. Farther north Fr Henry Francis Fitzsimmons had accompanied Lord Selkirk's expedition from Scotland to Prince Edward Island in 1803 and then on to Glengarry.

Rome now considered the development of the Church in the USA and Michael Egan was appointed the first bishop of Philadelphia in 1808. He struggled valiantly against serious difficulties until his death in 1814. At this time Irish Franciscans from Newfoundland served in the USA or Canada for varying periods of time. For example Ambrose Fitzpatrick was in Prince Edward Island and New Brunswick before going to Boston in 1818. After Bishop Egan's death it was decided to appoint another Irish friar as head of the Order in the USA. Fr Michael McCormick, another of the friars who helped save St Isidore's College, was chosen in 1815. However, he remained in Italy.

Charles Maguire was born near Enniskillen in 1768 and received the name Bonaventure when he joined the Franciscans at St Anthony's College, Louvain. During his studies he became friendly with Fr James McCormick, brother of Michael, and joined both brothers at St Isidore's College, Rome, in 1793. He lectured in philosophy and theology until forced to flee to Gratz in Austria following the French invasion of Rome. By the time Napoleon was defeated at Waterloo Fr Maguire had acquired a substantial income, and was fluent in French, German and Italian. However, many of his family had emigrated to Pennsylvania in the USA and he decided to go there as a missionary. In addition to the normal faculties, he was empowered by the minister general 'to introduce our holy Order into North America'. Towards the end of 1817 he arrived in Philadelphia but soon moved to the Pittsburg area and took up residence at Sportsman's Hall where Fr Lonergan had worked. Without his 79 knowledge he was proposed for the diocese of Charleston by Fr James Cowan, who had himself refused the honour. In 1822 Fr Maguire tried to establish a friary on a 113 acre site near Pittsburg. At one end of the property he built a two-storey log house to accommodate a maximum of six friars and a log chapel. At the other end a log cabin was erected for Poor Clare Sisters. Due to a lack of vocations the venture lasted only two years but it was the first Franciscan friary to be established in North America since the time of the Spanish friars in California. Fr Maguire continued to work in western Pennsylvania and was appointed vicar general of the area. He was also recommended for various bishoprics. He died in 1833.

John Daly came from near Athlone and received the name Benedict when he joined the Franciscans in 1828. In 1837 he presented himself to Bishop Fenwick of Boston and was given charge of the southern part of Vermont. The only priest in the area, he served twelve outstations based in Castleton and Middlebury. In spite of many obstacles he established the Catholic faith in a large area of the present diocese of Burlington. In 1854 he retired to New York where he met the Italian Franciscans who had just arrived to found what eventually became the province of the Immaculate Conception. Fr Daly died in 1872. The last Irish Franciscan to have an impact in the USA in the nineteenth century was Fr P. J. Cuddihy, who worked in the diocese of Springfield from 1852 until his death in 1898. Since the Second World War a number of Irish friars have worked in the USA for extended periods, mostly engaged in specialized work in such areas as the mass media, retreats, or parish ministry.

## Irish Franciscans in Australia

The first Irish Franciscan missionary departed for Australia in 1838 while Fr Hughes was Provincial. However, the first Irish friar associated with the provision of priests for Australia was Fr Richard Hayes. Following the receipt of information from his elder brother, who had been living in the country for seventeen years, Fr Hayes petitioned Rome for priests in 1816, and Fr Jeremiah Flynn, o.cist, was assigned to the Australian mission. The official attitude of opposition to the presence of Catholic clergy lessened and a number of priests, many of them English Benedictines, were recruited.

During a trip to Europe Fr Ullathorne, then vicar general of Sydney, recruited a number of Irish priests. Many of these were secular, but two of them were Irish Franciscans. Fr Patrick (Bonaventure) Geoghegan ofm left Ireland in November 1838 and travelled to Australia with Fr Ullathorne. Initially he worked in the Melbourne region but later became the second bishop of Adelaide

(1859-64). Fr Nicholas Coffey went to Australia in 1842 and worked mainly in Sydney and at Parramatta until his death in 1857. The pattern of individual friars going to help in particular areas continued. Fr Patrick (Bonaventure) Sheil, who arrived to work in Melbourne in 1853, was appointed bishop of Adelaide in 1864, in succession to Dr Geoghegan. Dr Sheil died in 1872.

As yet there was no Franciscan community in Australia, but in 1871 Dr Sheil hoped to establish a foundation where the friars could live a proper community life. Fr Peter (Francis) O'Farrell had been working energetically towards this end. Born in Co. Longford in 1809, he entered the Order at St Isidore's, Rome, in 1832. He was commissary visitator of the Irish province in 1852 and sought to reform the friars in Ireland. He went to Australia in 1854 and worked mainly in the diocese of Sydney. From then until his death, while on holiday in Ireland in 1874, he encouraged every move for a permanent Franciscan community in Australia. In particular he raised money for this purpose.

Soon after Fr O'Farrell's death, Dr Roger Bede Vaughan, coadjutor to the archbishop of Sydney, opened negotiations for a foundation in the archdiocese. The Irish provincial definitory agreed in principle in 1876, but it was March 1879 before the first two friars, Frs Peter (James) Hanrahan and Martin (Augustine) Holohan, set sail. The final agreement was not signed until 6 June 1879. The community, based in Waverly, soon increased to six friars. From Waverly they staffed two residences, at Paddington and Woolahara.

The number of friars in Australia increased very slowly. By 1908 there were still only nine friars (including two on secondment from the English province), but the first Australian students were near ordination. Despite appeals for more missionaries it was not until after the First World War that friars began to arrive in greater numbers. In the interval disputes continued between the archbishop of Sydney and the friars concerning the future of the Franciscan area, a large section of the south east suburbs of the city. Eventually it was subdivided and taken away from the friars because they could not cope with the increasing population.

Permission had been granted for a novitiate in Australia in 1915 but it did not open. Between 1916 and 1925 attempts were made to run a seraphic college at Rydal for boys interested in joining the Franciscan Order. The Franciscan mission in Australia then consisted of the three original houses in Sydney to which a house in Brisbane was added later. In 1927 Fr Fidelis Griffin was appointed commissary provincial and quickly established the framework for a Franciscan education system. A seraphic college with twelve students opened in January 1928 and had thirty-five students the following year. A novitiate with five novices opened in 1930 and a student house in 1932. It was no longer necessary for aspirants to undertake the long journey to Europe. The scattered houses in Australia and New Zealand were erected into the Franciscan province of the Holy Spirit on 31 October 1939. The New Zealand mission was started by the Italian Franciscans. The first Irish friar to help there was James (Anthony) Mahoney in 1867. Difficulties with Bishop Croke, later archbishop of Cashel, forced the Franciscans to leave, but they returned to Auckland in 1937. In 1939 there were only 123 religious in the new province, which had eight houses. Nevertheless they undertook a very successful mission in New Guinea in 1949. Because of the Second World War, arrangements for the full transfer of authority from the Irish friars were not completed until 1949. However, a number of Irish friars remained in Australia until 1972.

## Mission of Suihsien, China

At the Eucharistic Congress in Dublin in 1932 the delegate general for China, Fr Gerard Lunter ofm, met the Irish provincial and discussed the possibility of an Irish Franciscan mission to China. Due to the great increase in vocations in Ireland which it was feared would stretch the resources of the Irish friaries to their limit, the provincial readily agreed to the idea. He consulted Fr Maurice Connaughton, a member of the Irish province who had been ordained in Hankow in 1913 and afterwards worked in China. On his recommendation it was agreed in March 1935 to accept an offer from Bishop Eugenio Massi, vicar of Hankow and an Italian Franciscan. The Irish would take over four administrative regions in the province of Hupeh, the main city being Suihsien and the others Yingshan and Anlu, the nearest to Hankow.

Seven Irish friars arrived at Shanghai on 18 December 1935 where they were joined by Fr Connaughton as head of the mission. The group took up residence in Anlu to learn Chinese. They had their initial pastoral experience in the summer of 1936, and also met bandits for the first time. At the end of the year they were joined by three companions who went to study Chinese in Peking. Early in 1937 the minister general agreed that the Irish section of the vicariate could become independent. On 17 June 1937 the Sacred Congregation of Propaganda Fide officially erected the new Prefecture Apostolic of Suihsien, with Mgr Connaughton as prefect. He was officially installed on 4 October 1937. At that time there were four Irish friars studying in Peking, one acting as procurator in Hong Kong, and six (including the prefect) in the prefecture along with two Italian friars and two Chinese secular priests. A year later Mgr Connaughton reported to Rome that missionaries were living at eight stations and serving thirty-five christianities (outstations). A minor seminary was functioning at Anlu and work had begun on the construction of a residence for the prefect at Suihsien. The residence was never occupied due to the outbreak of war. The Japanese who had maintained a puppet state in Manchuria since 1931, used the Marco Polo bridge incident of July 1937 as an excuse to renew hostilities. As the war escalated the Japanese advanced through the eastern end of the prefecture on their approach to Hankow. The friars set up official and unofficial refugee camps to cope with the thousands who fled in panic. Anlu fell in October 1938 and the front stabilized a little to the east of Suihsien during the winter of 1938-9. Suihsien fell in the spring of 1939 and the situation remained unchanged for the next six years. One mission station, Liaochiatsai, which was in the Chinese controlled area, continued to function normally. Contact with Ireland was still possible. Life continued more or less normally in the Japanese area, with refugee camps operating under the tricolour, until the Japanese attack on Pearl Harbour. The Japanese froze bank accounts in February 1942 and in April arrested all the missionaries, except those in Anlu. The six missionaries were placed under house arrest in the Franciscan College at Chiaokow, outside Hankow. Three friars who had been in Peking were trapped in north China. Two of the Irish friars went to Shanghai in the hope of escaping from China. In February 1944 three of the friars from Chiaokow joined Mgr Connaughton, two Irish friars and two Chinese priests in Anlu where they were confined within the missionary compound for nearly a year. An attempt to resume missionary activity early in 1945 was unsuccessful. Only after the end of the war in the Pacific in August 1945 could the missionaries return to their stations.

The conflict between Communists and Nationalists which had been dormant during the fight against the Japanese re-emerged as a full-scale civil war late in 1945. The strain of the war years and house arrest had taken its toll, and several friars who were no longer fit for missionary duty had to be sent back to Europe. In 1947 all the missions were functioning and a total of twelve priests, not all Irish, were active. In August five new priests and five sisters of the Franciscan Missionaries of the Divine Motherhood arrived. In the same month Communist forces invaded the prefecture and by Christmas all except Anlu was under their control. Given the experiences of foreign missionaries in other areas, the Irish friars were ordered to withdraw since it was anticipated that the Nationalists would return and win the war with American help. In 1948 this help was discontinued in the belief that such a move would force both sides to negotiate a peace. The result was a Communist victory. On the instructions of the Franciscan delegate general most of the Irish friars fled while the Chinese, one diocesan priest and three Franciscans, went underground. Mgr Connaughton and a companion remained in Anlu to maintain a Catholic presence in the area but were placed under house arrest. Because of health problems they withdrew to join another friar in Hankow in the summer of 1950. The younger friar was diagnosed as seriously ill and got permission to go to Hong Kong in December. The authorities in Rome ordered Mgr Connaughton to resign, which he did. He left Hankow on Good Friary 1951 and spent his remaining years in California where he died in 1967. Fr Dominic Ch'en ofm was appointed to replace him. He was shot by Red guards in Hankow probably in 1970. The last Irish Franciscan was ordered to leave Hankow in December 1951. In 1950 an Irish friar took charge of the Franciscan procuration in Hong Kong. This had been under Irish control from 1936 until 1939. He remained there until 1957, during which time its main function was the reception of expelled missionaries.

### Activities in South Africa

The Irish province had been unable to send out missionaries during the Second World War, although a number of friars served as chaplains in Europe, the Far East and North Africa. By 1946 there were a number of volunteers eager to work as missionaries in distant lands. Two were sent to staff the College of St Albert, Ernakulam, Cochin, India, in 1947, but were soon forced to retire due to difficult conditions. Five new missionaries went to China, but that mission soon closed. However, the main Irish effort was directed towards South Africa.

Bishop Fleischer of Marianhill invited German Franciscans from his native Bavaria to help him in 1932. Their initial efforts were too dispersed and in 1935 they decided to concentrate on the area around Kokstad. This was erected into the prefecture apostolic of Mount Currie in 1935 with an ex-Chinese missionary, Fr Sigebald Kurz ofm, as prefect. It was raised to a vicariate in 1939 and Fr Kurz was consecrated bishop by Pius XII. The bishop and all except four of the missionaries were interned as enemy aliens during the Second World War. Bishop Kurz resigned in 1945 and the apostolic delegate to South Africa, Archbishop Martin Lucas, whose secretary was an Irish friar, Fr Urban O'Sullivan, invited the Irish Franciscans to take over. They agreed and the first four missionaries, accompanied by the minister provincial, arrived in Kokstad on 27 December 1946. Three more arrived the following year. The provincial, Fr Evangelist McBride, decided to join them and was consecrated bishop of Ezani on 25 July 1949. On 11 January 1951 Bishop McBride became head of the new diocese of Kokstad with the erection of the hierarchy in South Africa. There were then about 4,500 Catholics out of a population of just under 400,000, mainly Xhosa, in the diocese. It was staffed by twenty-three priests, thirteen Irish, nine German and an Austrian and by six brothers, two Irish and four German. They were helped by seventy nuns, fifty catechists and eighty teachers in the eleven mission stations and seventy-six outstations. Bishop McBride retired in 1978 and was replaced by Bishop Wilfrid Napier, a native of the diocese who had joined the Franciscans and studied in Ireland and Belgium, and later became president of the South African Episcopal Conference. Soon after taking over the diocese he reported a Catholic population of nearly 45,000 out of a total of 925,000 people being served by eighteen Franciscans, forty-seven nuns and one hundred and twenty-seven catechists.

Archbishop Lucas also invited the Irish Franciscans to staff a seminary for white clerics – this was before the Nationalist Party came to power in 1948 with their policy of racial segregation. Two Irish friars arrived and opened a temporary seminary at Queenstown, near Port Elizabeth, on 14 April 1948. The foundation stone of a permanent building was laid on 26 February 1950 in Pretoria, and the new seminary opened there on 1 March 1951. It developed rapidly and soon had a staff of twelve. In 1977 a decision was taken to desegregate the seminary despite its location in a white area. By 1980 there were sixty-five students, forty-seven of whom were residential. Of the sixty-five students, thirty were white, fifteen black, eleven coloured, three Indian and one Chinese. By 1984 the college was overcrowded, attempting to cater for seventy-five residential and twenty-two non-residential students. A decision was taken to move the faculty of philosophy to Hammanskrall in 1985. The theology faculty remained in Pretoria. However, the seminary is again approaching its maximum capacity.

The bishop of Johannesburg invited the Irish to take over some parishes in the district of Vereeniging and the first friars arrived there in 1955. This district contains parishes in both black and white areas of the Vaal Triangle. The provincial house for the Order in South Africa is at Vanderbijlpark, which is a white parish. To the east of it is the white parish of Vereeniging. The retreat centre of La Verna at Barrage Farm is in the countryside to the west. The friars main area of pastoral activity is to the north in the large black townships of Sharpeville, Sebokeng, Evaton and Residensia. Their work includes saying mass in a converted garage, designing and building a new church, and teaching catechism and confirmation classes. They are active in campaigns for social justice in cases such as that of the Sharpeville Six. The friars came to Boksburg in Johannesburg to run a minor seminary. In 1965 a new coloured township called Reiger Park was set up and a friar sent there to take pastoral charge. He set up a small library in the township. In 1970 a nun joined the mission to take charge of education. A school and church were built. Rapid expansion followed. The complex now provides medical facilities, a day-centre, a language laboratory and a computer centre. Over 5,000 students attend each year.

Other Franciscan groups operating in South Africa included Bavarians in Kokstad and English friars in Ermelo and Volksrust. A number of South Africans came to Europe to enter the Order, but distance and expense made the Fransiscan authorities discourage others from following. As fewer friars from Europe were interested in going to an increasingly troubled South Africa, the Franciscans there began to make their own arrangements. The Franciscan Federation of Southern Africa was erected in February 1977. A novitiate was set up at Besters in 1980 followed by a student house at the Kraal outside Pretoria in 1980 and a pre-novitiate in 1982. A number of local young men joined the Order. Under the Federation the friars in South Africa had initially remained members of their home provinces. The next step was complete amalgamation and the vice-province of Our Lady Queen of Peace in Southern Africa was erected on 12 April 1985 with eighty solemnly professed friars and ten in simple vows. Of these, forty, including the provincial, were Irish.

## Zimbabwe Mission

Early in 1958 two Irish Franciscans went to Salisbury and a contract was signed with the archbishop of Salisbury in July allowing the friars to take over the parish of Waterfalls. In May of the following year the friars agreed to take over the Charter and Buhera districts in the country to the south of the capital. The friary at Waterfalls opened in April 1960 and in November the first friars moved into the rural mission area. The new mission expanded slowly during the 1960s despite the tensions caused by the declaration of UDI in Rhodesia in 1965. By 1975 the mission consisted of a friary at Waterfalls and eight mission stations in the country district staffed by nearly twenty friars. The civil war of the late 1970s greatly disrupted the mission. Three friars were expelled and several suffered serious psychological problems which necessitated their return to Ireland. At one stage the number of missionaries was reduced to four.

The war ended in 1980 with Rhodesia becoming the new state of Zimbabwe and Salisbury being re-named Harare. Ten friars were then staffing the friary in Harare and three of the eight country missions. A local young man had entered the Order and was studying in Ireland and was soon followed by a second student. A novitiate has since been set up in Zimbabwe and three novices have been simply professed. Bringing the number of Irish missionaries up to previous levels presented more difficulties. By 1987 thirteen priests and two brothers were running two houses in Harare, and five country mission stations. The Poor Clares had also established a monastery in Harare. Zimbabwe is now the only mission directly dependent on the Irish province.

## Latin America

Pope John XXIII appealed for priests to look after the spiritually undernourished Catholic people of Latin America. In response to his appeal one Irish Franciscan went to Chile in 1964 to help the Chilean Franciscans. A second group joined him in April 1968. By 1972 the friars were involved in three parishes. Three Irish priests, one of whom was parish priest, were working with a Chilean priest and two brothers in a parish of about 45,000 people in Santiago, the capital. Two Irish priests and a Chilean brother were ministering in the country parish of Rapel which had a population of 7,000. A Chilean priest and a brother who also lived there ran a small agricultural college. Two Irish priests and an aged Chilean priest served the urban-rural parish of Limache in the diocese of Valparaiso, where the church had been severely damaged by an earthquake. It was decided to close the mission on 1 June 1977. One friar remained behind until he was expelled by the government in 1983.

A number of Irish friars became interested in ministering in Bolivia at the time the Chilean mission closed. By 1979 three were working in La Paz, but when the mission was not granted official status two left. The third remained teaching in a seminary until 1988. A few individual friars worked in other parts of Latin America. However, the only other official Irish Franciscan Mission was in El Salvador.

Central America originally had two Franciscan provinces but both were suppressed in 1922. Over the next fifty years six provinces sent missionaries to the region, and the last to arrive were the Irish. Following contact between the archbishop of San Salvador and the Irish Franciscans it was agreed that the friars would take over the parish of Gotera in the diocese of San Miguel. The parish was in a rugged country district with dirt roads and many rivers, and had a Catholic population of 65,000. The first Irish friars arrived in 1968 and a community of four lived there for the next decade. By then civil unrest in the country was escalating. The friars tried to form basic Christian communities as outlined in the Medellin documents. By the end of the 1970s there were 300 trained catechists/leaders and four vocations to the Franciscan Order. The closure of the mission in

87

Chile and the withdrawal of friars from Bolivia made additional resources available for the mission in El Salvador. The friars agreed to take over the parish of Our Lady Queen of Peace, Soyapango. By the beginning of 1984 there were nine Irish priests and two Irish deacons in El Salvador. A major Franciscan reorganization was undertaken. In 1974 the minister general had erected a federation of the various Franciscan missions in Central America. Following extensive consultation it was decided to join all the missions in these countries into the Vicariate of Our Lady of Guadalupe, with effect from 12 December 1983. While a number of Italian and Spanish missionaries opted to remain independent, the Irish entered into the new unit enthusiastically. The friars still work at Gotera and Soyapango, and at Carrizal, a rural zone, and Concepcion, an inner-city parish in San Salvador.

Zimbabwe is now the only Irish Franciscan mission. However, the province remains committed to supporting the friars in the new independent units in South Africa and El Salvador.

Individual friars continue to work in various parts of the world, such as England and the USA. Since their first missionary undertaking to Newfoundland in the 1780s, the contribution of the Irish Franciscans to the foreign missions, especially in this century, has been impressive.

*Monster, Waterford Friary*

# Chapter 6

# THE LARGER IRISH FRANCISCAN FAMILY

The main concern of this book is with the history of the Order of Friars Minor in Ireland. However, this chapter will look at those religious in other Orders and congregations who trace their origins back to St Francis of Assisi. The Franciscan family is divided into three Orders: the First Order for men, the Second Order for women, and the Third Order, which was initially for the laity. The First Order is composed of three independent Orders, each with equal rights and privileges: the Friars Minor, the Friars Minor Conventual, and the Friars Minor Capuchins. The Second Order in Ireland, the Poor Clares, called after St Clare of Assisi, is composed of two independent groups, both of whom have a common origin. The Third Order Regular, comprising those religious who base their lives on the rule written by St Francis for the laity, is made up of a large number of congregations.

## The Friars Minor Conventual

A reform movement developed in the fifteenth century which resulted in the Franciscan Order splitting into two in 1517. The main focus of this book has been on the Irish Observants. The Conventuals ceased to exist in Ireland in the second half of the sixteenth century. However, Irishmen continued to join the Conventuals outside of Ireland. The Conventuals returned to England in 1907 when Fr Bonaventure Scerberras took over a parish near Bristol. By 1955 there were six Conventual houses accommodating forty friars in England. These were then erected into a province.

The Conventuals, who have always been involved in parish work, began to negotiate with Archbishop McNamara of Dublin with a view to returning to Ireland. He gave his consent and in the 1980s the first Conventual friars came to work in individual parishes while arrangements were made for them to take over a parish of their own. They took control of the parish of Fairview in 1986.

## The Friars Minor Capuchins

Irish Capuchin history begins with Fr Francis Nugent (better known as Friar Nugent), 1569-1635. From Moyrath in Co. Meath, he joined the Capuchins in Brussels. Despite indifference by the general chapter he succeeded in obtaining a papal brief from Paul V to erect an Irish Capuchin Mission and was himself appointed as commissary general on 29 May 1608. After houses at Lille (1610) and Cologne (1611), he erected the mother-house of the Irish province at Charleville in 1615, in which year Fr Stephen Daly was the first Capuchin sent to Ireland. He was soon followed by Fr Laurence Nugent. Two more friars came in 1618. During his first visit home, in 1624, Friar Nugent was given the use of a house outside Newgate in Dublin which became the first canonical foundation. The other religious Orders in the city opposed the new arrivals. Their opposition continued for some years and was exacerbated by the transfer of a number of Friars Minor to the Capuchins.

The number of foundations rose rapidly. By 1642 there were fifty-one friars on the mission in Ireland. In addition to Dublin, foundations had been made at Cork, Drogheda, Limerick, Mullingar and Slane. Further houses were set up at Athy, Clonmel, Galway, Swords and Thurles, some of which were extremely small and may never have consisted of more than one or two friars. Like other religious, the Capuchins suffered grievously in the Cromwellian period. Many of their early foundations were closed but the number of friars remained stable. In 1685 the house at Charleville was replaced by two others in France: Bar-sur-Aube and Vassy in Champagne. Up to their suppression in 1793, these two houses remained central to the Irish Capuchin Mission. The provincial lived in France, the Chapters were held there, novices and students were trained there and many of the friars never returned to Ireland. Some remarked that the Irish province was more French than Irish. There were only three foundations in Ireland during most of the eighteenth century, with no more than thirty Capuchins living in the country.

The Irish Capuchin Mission had been formally erected without members in 1608, and became a custody in 1698. The province of St Patrick was erected on 22 September 1733, with Fr Philip O'Kennedy as minister provincial. Efforts to extend the Irish Mission to Scotland and the Isle of Man towards the end of the seventeenth century failed.

The effects of the French Revolution were catastrophic for the Irish Capuchins whose principal base was in France. The Irish province was reduced to a General Commissariate in 1855. By then there were only about twelve Capuchins left in Ireland. In two stages, in 1864 and 1866 all foundations of the Order in Ireland and England were gathered into a single custody. The friars, like their Franciscan counterparts, had begun to move away from living as secular priests. The Order was developing in England and in 1873 the English houses and two Irish houses, Cork and Rochestown, were erected into a full province. The two remaining Irish houses, Dublin and Kilkenny, became an independent custody under the supervision of the provincial of Paris. The Irish opposed this and petitioned Rome for change. A novitiate was set up in Kilkenny in 1875 which was transferred to Rochestown two years later. A seraphic school was erected in Kilkenny in 1884. Following a general chapter of the Order held in 1884 it was decided that the four houses in Ireland, including friars from several other nationalities, could once again be erected into a full province. This was done by a papal decree of 21 January 1885 which named Fr Seraphin of Bruges as the new provincial.

The Capuchins shared in the general growth of religious Orders in Ireland during the first part of the twentieth century. The Irish province of the Capuchins now has over a hundred members in twelve houses in Ireland, five in Dublin, four in Cork, one each in Kilkenny, Carlow and Donegal. There is a vice-province on the Pacific coast of the USA, a district in New Zealand and missions in Zambia and South Africa. About half of the total of three hundred friars live in Ireland.

## The Second Order of St Francis: The Poor Clares

In most countries, the Second Order developed along with the First Order. The first Poor Clare foundation in England was made at Northampton in 1252. There is no evidence for the Second Order in Ireland until 1629. Such a community may have existed, especially following the Observant and Colettine reforms in the fifteenth century, but if it did, no record of it remains.

Several Irish girls travelled to the Continent early in the seventeenth century and joined various Poor Clare convents. English nuns had set up an English Poor Clare Convent at Gravelines in 1607. This English foundation became a natural centre for Irish girls wishing to join the Order. The first known Irish Poor Clare is Sr Martha Marianna Cheevers, and she inspired a group of five nuns to establish an Irish Poor Clare convent at Dunkirk in 1625. This foundation was not a success. On the advice of the Irish Franciscans at Louvain, the nuns moved to Nieuport in 1627.

In June 1629 the first group of Poor Clares led by Mother Cecily of St Francis Dillon, arrived in Ireland. In August the Franciscan friars meeting in Chapter at Limerick officially welcomed them. After the tolerant Lord Deputy, Falkland, had been recalled a period of persecution ensued, during which the sisters in Dublin, who had attracted twelve postulants, were arrested on 22 October 1630.

Released on parole, they left Dublin and set up a convent at 'Bethlehem', Co. Westmeath. The ruins of their building can still be seen by the shores of Lough Ree, five miles north of Athlone. After ten    91 years the community numbered sixty sisters. A new foundation was made at Drogheda in 1639. 'Bethlehem' was sacked by an English army in May 1642. The community escaped, some to join a small group of sisters who had made a foundation in Galway in January 1642, others to Wexford, Waterford and Athlone.

On 10 July 1649 Galway Corporation presented Nuns' Island to the Poor Clares. They were forced to flee during the Cromwellian period, but returned to Galway in 1660. Expelled again in 1690, they set up their community in Market Square. In 1825 they returned to Nuns' Island.

Following a series of reforms, they went back to the strict obser-vance of the 'Colettine' life on 16 July 1892. In 1893 a group of Poor Clares from Levenshulme, near Manchester, under Mother Mary Seraphine Bowe, landed at Drogheda on their way to make a found-ation at Graigue, Carlow, at the invitation of the bishop, Dr Lynch. In 1906 seven sisters left Carlow and established a new foundation at Donnybrook. In 1924 a group from Donnybrook founded a house in Belfast.

Sr Maria Dwyer of Cork had been professed at Tournai in Belgium. Helped by the bishop of Cork and by her father, she and another sister established a new foundation in Cork on Christmas Day 1914. Four sisters came from Carlow to join them. As the community in Cork grew, plans were made for a foundation in Ennis. The first stone was laid on 17 September 1957, and the sisters left Cork for their new home on 8 November 1958.

The Irish Poor Clares also founded houses in other countries. The Galway house helped to found Southampton in 1934 and Sydney in 1951. Similarly Donnybook helped establish Neath in 1950, Cork helped found Bothwell in 1952 and Ennis Campbelltown in 1971. Most recently the Irish houses helped in the foundation at Harare.

Two converts from Anglicanism, Elizabeth Sophia Law and Mary Anne Hayes, were received into the Catholic Church in 1851. With a companion they went to Paris and became Franciscan Third Order Regular nuns. In 1854, following their return to London, they set up the congregation of the Franciscan Sisters of Perpetual Adoration. With the help of the Ram family, the sisters came to Gorey in 1858, but were unable to establish a permanent foundation. Eventually a community of nine founded a house at Drumshanbo, on 8 December 1864. A second, short-lived, foundation was made at Drumsna on 8 August 1918.

Following Vatican II, it was suggested that the Poor Clare houses in Ireland be organized into a federation. On 14 April 1973 the Irish houses, together with the three English houses, formed a federation governed by a federal abbess residing in Galway. Common constitutions were drafted and a unified formation programme was brought into existence by which all novices would spend some time training in Galway. In August 1973 the Sisters of Perpetual Adoration at Drumshanbo decided to join the federation of Galway, Ennis, Cork, Carlow, Donnybrook, Belfast, Southampton, Neath and Bothwell.

## The Sisters of St Clare

At the beginning of the eighteenth century Galway was the only Poor Clare foundation left in Ireland. At the request of Archbishop Edmund Byrne of Dublin six Poor Clares left Galway in 1712 and moved to Dublin, settling initially in Channel Row before moving to North King Street in 1715. In 1751-2 the community split into two groups and a new house was established, in Russell's Court. The original group in North King Street founded a school for young girls. Later they moved to Dun Laoghaire and the foundation ceased to exist in the 1830s. The new group transferred from Russell's Court to Dorset Street. Here they took over an orphanage in 1803. As the building proved unsuitable they decided to build a new house in Harold's Cross. In 1804 papal permission for a new rule was granted. The new orphanage was opened in 1806.

The sisters hoped to make a second foundation in Dundrum but were unsuccessful and instead founded a house in Newry in 1830. Here they ran a school. Newry became a centre for a series of foundations in Ulster. A national school was set up in Cavan in 1861, and a second school established in Ballyjamesduff in 1872. From Newry, schools were also founded in Keady in 1871 and Mayobridge in 1922. A school was set up in Kenmare in 1861, and the sisters sent a mission to Sydney, Australia, in 1883.

In 1944 the mother house in Newry and its five daughter foundations petitioned the Holy See for permission to amalgamate. A papal decree was issued and Mother Mary Agnes O'Brien was elected first abbess general. Subsequently all the houses originating from Newry, except Waverly, joined the amalgamation and other new houses were founded. At a chapter held in 1970 it was decided to divide the Order into regions. The general chapter of 1973 decided that the congregation would be known as the Sisters of St Clare to avoid confusion with the Poor Clares. By then Waverly had joined the amalgamation and in 1975, the original community in Harold's Cross also joined. The Sisters define their role as bringing the contemplative charisma of St Clare to the world through varied ministries. In 1985 the Irish region consisted of eighteen communities, the English region of thirteen communities, the American region of seven communities and the Central American region of three houses.

## Franciscan Third Order Regular (Mediaeval)

The ideals of the Franciscan Third Order Secular have led many to take up the religious life. In mediaeval times groups of tertiaries began to come together to form regular communities. The concept of a defined religious congregation began to emerge in 1412 during the reign of the antipope John XXIII. It would seem from decrees of Pope Martin V in 1425 and 1426 that there were Third Order Regular communities in Ireland by that date. These were communities of men. There is some evidence for communities of women at a later date, but they never became very prominent.

The first foundation was at Killeenbrenan near Shrule in Co. Mayo *c.* 1426, and the next at Clonkeenkerrill, east Galway, *c.* 1435. These were followed by many foundations in the Gaelic areas of the west and north. The brothers initially depended on priests of the First Order for services but later ordained some of their own members. The structure of the Third Order Regular was that of a loose federation. They were chiefly concerned with education, prayer and a life of Franciscan witness.

By 1450 the Third Order Regular had twelve houses. This number increased to thirty-six by 1500 and to forty at the time of the Suppression. With very few exceptions, they were concentrated in Ulster and Connacht. Structurally the Third Order houses vary greatly. Some resemble miniature First Order friaries, for example Rosserk is similar to nearby Moyne. Others consist of a simple church with residence attached, such as Friarstown. Being comparatively late, the buildings are good examples of reticulated or flamboyant style.

Since the houses of the Third Order were usually in isolated areas, they survived the early stages of the Suppression. About twelve communities survived the Elizabethan persecutions. Most of these were in mid-Ulster and enjoyed protection by the local chiefs. After the Flight of the Earls they were gradually suppressed.

## Franciscan Third Order Regular (Modern)

In 1817 a group of zealous men, members of the Third Order Secular attached to Merchant's Quay Friary, Dublin, came together and took religious vows. Their director was Fr John (Francis) Dunne ofm They opened three schools to educate the poor, one at Milltown, and two in Dalkey, Co. Dublin.

In 1818 Christopher Dillon Bellew, with the approval of Dr Kelly, archbishop of Tuam, invited the brothers to open a school at Mountbellew, Co. Galway. They went to Mountbellew but the foundation stone of the permanent building was not laid until 1823. The schools near Dublin were eventually closed and the official name of the new congregation became 'The Franciscan Brothers of the

Third Order Regular, Mountbellew'. They remained under the control of the First Order until the passing of Catholic Emancipation in 1829. Fearing the consequences of the restrictions contained in the Emancipation Bill, they petitioned the Holy See to be placed under the jurisdiction of the archbishop of Tuam. This was granted in 1830 and, under the protection of Dr MacHale, they expanded rapidly in the west, hence their popular name, 'Monks of the West'.

Mountbellew became the base for expansion to such places as Clifden, Roundstone, Errew, Tourmakeady, Achill, Cummer, Granlahan, Kilkerrin and Annadown. Another Franciscan group was set up at Clara, and later made a foundation in conjunction with Mountbellew at Farragher. This loose federation was united by a decree of Pope Benedict XV on 5 February 1918 and was erected into a full pontifical brotherhood on 21 June 1938. At present the brothers have eight houses in Ireland, three in the USA and two each in both Nigeria and the Cameroons.

## Franciscan Sisterhoods

Several Orders of nuns use the Third Order rule as a basis for their life, and are, effectively, the female equivalent of the Franciscan brothers.

The Franciscan Missionaries of Mary were founded in Madras, India, by Mother Mary of the Passion in 1877 and have Irish houses at Loughglynn, Co. Roscommon, Dublin, Belfast and Galway.

The Franciscan Missionaries of the Divine Motherhood were officially established in 1935 when Mother Mary Francis Spring led a group to found Mount Alverna Nursing Home at Guilford in England. Final papal approval was received in 1963. In Ireland their main foundation is the Portiuncula Hospital, Ballinasloe, with others at Dublin and Beaufort, Co. Kerry.

The Franciscan Missionary Sisters of St Joseph have houses at Dublin, Farranferris (Cork) and Freshford, Co. Kilkenny. They were founded at Mill Hill, London, in 1883 by Mother Mary Francis Ingham, with the help of Cardinal Vaughan.

The Franciscan Missionary Sisters for Africa have their generalate at Mount Oliver, Dundalk and a house of formation in Dublin. Founded in 1903, their first superior general was Mother Mary Kevin, 'Mama Kevina'.

The Franciscan Missionaries of Our Lady, known as Franciscan Sisters of Calais, ran a house in Dublin until 1965 and the Sacred Heart Hospital, Ballinderry, Co. Westmeath. This Order came into existence through an amalgamation of several Third Order houses in France in 1854.

The Franciscan Sisters of the Atonement, the female equivalent of the Graymoor Friars, run a hostel for the elderly at Rossinver in Co. Leitrim.

The Franciscan Sisters of the Immaculate Conception run a school at Falcarragh in Co. Donegal.

The Missionary Franciscan Sisters of the Immaculate Conception were founded by Mother Mary Ignatius Hayes at Belle Prairie in the USA in 1873 and their principal Irish house was at Bloomfield, Co. Westmeath, but is now in Dublin.

Also connected with the Franciscan family are the Sisters of the Holy Cross in Belfast. They were founded in Switzerland in 1844.

The Franciscan Sisters of Mill Hill were founded in London in 1868 by Sr Mary Francis Basil with five other Anglican Sisters. Their original house was Hope Castle, Castleblaney, but they now work in Dublin and Belfast.

## Anglican Franciscans

In 1921 a few men inspired by the example of St Francis settled near Batcombe in Dorset. Their aim was to share the life of the unemployed on the roads in England during the Depression. Three of them took vows before the bishop of Salisbury in 1931. They were joined by the Rev. Algy Robertson and others from the Brotherhood of the Love of Christ in 1936 and the Society of St Francis was formed.

Bishop Butler of Connor invited them to his diocese in 1972. The following year they opened a house near the peace line between the Shankill and the Falls Road in Belfast. Because of redevelopment, they had to move to Deerpark Road in 1976. In 1983 they were joined by two Sisters. Their work includes assisting in local parishes, serving as chaplains in Crumlin Road gaol, youth work, social work and teaching. They have also organized a small Anglican Franciscan Third Order which has members in many parts of Ireland.

*Decorative carving, Askeaton Friary, Co. Limerick*

# Chapter 7

# IRISH FRANCISCAN
# ARCHITECTURE AND ART

## The Mediaeval Period

The first Franciscans used existing buildings as residences and went
to local parish churches for services. Later they built their own
churches and extended their domestic quarters. By the beginning of
the fourteenth century they had begun to build friaries to an established plan.

In a typical mediaeval friary a narrow church ran east-west. The
main altar was at the eastern end, beneath a large and ornate east
window. This window was both practical, admitting the light of the
rising sun, and symbolic, the sun rising being a sign of the risen
Christ. The eastern end of the church served as a choir for the friars,
while the western end was a nave for the people. Pillars supported a
tall, slender tower dividing choir from nave. Between the pillars was
a small loft, usually of wood, known as the rood loft. This served as a
pulpit for preaching. The friars often built a small transept chapel,
usually containing two altars, to the south of the junction of tower
and nave. In a few cases an aisle was added to the south of the nave
itself.

Artistically, the most important feature of the church was the east
window. Window design underwent a continuous evolution. The
early mediaeval period, 1250-1350, was characterized by lancet
windows, or windows divided into lights, while the later mediaeval
period, 1400-1550, was characterized by the use of tracery in the
windows (see illustrations p. 98). Sculptured decorations can be found
around the main windows, both inside and out, and on corbels and
finials, especially underneath the tower. Important tombs, which
were often elaborately decorated, were situated in the choir.

The residential part of the friary usually consisted of three ranges
built around a cloister on the north side of the church. The east range
normally contained the sacristy and refectory, while the north range
contained the kitchen area. The dormitories, typified by small
narrow windows, were usually on the first floor above the kitchen and
the refectory, so that the heat from below would keep them warm.
The west range consisted of store-rooms and workshops. The three
ranges were normally connected by an ambulatory, the covered walk
around the central garden area, called 'the cloisters'. In early friaries 97

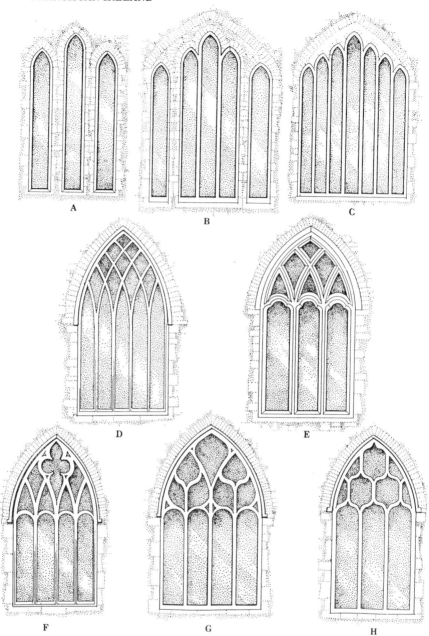

*Window styles: thirteenth to sixteenth centuries*

**A:** lancets, Waterford *c.* 1250. **B:** lancet and lancet lights, Ennis *c.* 1300. **C:** lancet-light groups, Kilkenny *c.* 1320. **D:** switch-line tracery, Askeaton *c.* 1430. **E:** switch-line-and-bar tracery, Quin *c.* 1460. **F:** switch-line with quartrefoil, Moyne *c.* 1470. **G:** flowing, Dromahair *c.* 1510. **H:** reticulated, Dromahair *c.* 1510.

the arcade of the ambulatory was usually free-standing, but in later friaries it often supports the wall of the dormitory. There is nearly always some trace of a stream flowing by the north range, both to supply fresh water and to take away sewage.

These central buildings were surrounded by a series of outhouses. The complex was entered through a gateway which had a niche for the patron saint. Where water was plentiful, there was always a mill, and in many cases a weir as well.

There is a large quantity of art associated with these mediaeval buildings. Cloister arcades, corbels and pillars can be highly decorated. Tombs of the fifteenth and early sixteenth century are often surrounded by representations of the saints, called 'weepers', who are supposed to be both in mourning and interceding for the dead person. In addition many mediaeval and seventeenth-century statues have survived.

This art shows a great richness of imaginative and technical achievement, ranging from the human head looking upward from a doorstep in Ennis, through the snipe and the monster with shamrock tail and long mediaeval shoes at Waterford, the collection of kings and servants under the tower in Kilkenny, and the owl gazing down from the side of the tower in Kilconnell. In other carvings a lady with a magnificent head-dress is reading in Ennis, three women look over the head of a bishop in Carrick-on-Suir, and three others, one with a decorated brooch, accompany a knight in Cashel. The suffering and death of Christ are widely portrayed. In Ennis there is a complete set of bas-reliefs representing the paschal mysteries, as well as an *Ecce Homo*, which shows the instruments of the Passion, ladder, nails, money, pliers, whip, sponge, and even the cock boiling in the pot, a theme repeated at Kilcullen and elsewhere. One of the most beautiful surviving items is the processional cross from Lislaughtin now in the National Museum, Dublin. An early drawing of the seal of the province dating to the fifteenth century, also survives. The statues from the late mediaeval and seventeenth-century period include eight from Waterford, which are now in private hands, two from Adare, one of which is in Multyfarnham friary, while the other is in Cork Museum, and the statue of Our Lady of Bethlehem which is now in Galway. A damaged Madonna from Askeaton, the head of a Madonna from Kilconnell and pieces of a cross from Kilcrea, also survive.

The representations of St Francis will be considered as exemplifying Irish Franciscan art. The earliest example is probably that above the doorway built by Dean Odo O'Malone before 1459 on the north wall of the cathedral in Clonmacnois. Dating from the same period is the figure of the saint carved as part of the surround of a now-

*Corbel figures, Kilkenny Friary*

vanished tomb in Ennis. A portrayal of St Francis was carved on one
of the cloister pillars in Askeaton. The features of the face have been
worn away as a result of the local belief that kissing the figure is a cure
for toothache. At nearby Adare a bas-relief of the saint was inserted
into the cloister wall. A wooden statue of him from the same friary has
also survived. In Kilconnell there is a figure of St Francis beside an
unidentified bishop on top of a mid-fifteenth century tomb. Roland
FitzEustace, baron of Portlester, erected a tomb for himself and his
wife at the friary which they had founded in Kilcullen. The tomb,
featuring a representation of St Francis, still stands in the graveyard.
In St Werburgh's Church, Dublin, there is a figure of St Francis on
the side of a Purcell tomb dating to the early sixteenth century. At
Meelick in Co. Galway there is a bas-relief of the saint which proba-

bly came from the cloister of the friary. A representation of him is also
found on the side of a tomb in the priory of the Canons Regular of St
Augustine at Mothel in Co. Waterford. There are two representations of the saint on the side of a pillar in the cloister at Dromahair,
Co. Leitrim, which dates to the 1530s. Finally, there is a large statue
of the saint in the friary at Carrickbeg, in which he is shown wearing
the collar of a fisherman's tunic. The statue is probably a piece of
folk-art of the late eighteenth century. A figure on the side of a tomb
which dates to 1557 in the cathedral of St Carthage, Lismore, is
sometimes identified as St Francis but seems to lack the stigmata.

All known representations show the stigmata on St Francis' right
side, visible through the open habit. Most show the saint pointing to
the stigmata with one hand while the other is raised in blessing. The

wound on the raised hand is usually visible, that on the other hand occasionally so. In a small group of representations (Ennis, Kilconnell, Meelick and the lower of the two figures in Dromahair), one hand is beside the wound in the saint's side while the other holds or touches a cross, which is not a symbol of the Passion but resembles the staff carried by itinerant preachers. The feet are not generally visible, except at Ennis and Askeaton where the wounds in the feet can be seen. The cord, usually with three knots symbolizing the three vows of religious life, is always present.

In the areas under English influence St Francis is generally shown with a severe expression, while in the Gaelic areas he is often represented with a more cheerful countenance, as at Kilconnell, Meelick and Dromahair where he is depicted preaching to the birds and the leaves from a pulpit which is also a flower with a stem incorporating two Irish knots.

## Sixteenth- to Nineteenth-Century Architecture

During the second half of the sixteenth century, as the Tudor reconquest progressed, the friars were driven out of their friaries in the areas conquered by English armies, and forced to live in places of refuge, usually cottages in obscure places. By 1612 the number of friaries still inhabited had been reduced to eight of which four were the original mediaeval sites. Some old sites were re-occupied during the seventeenth century. Despite harassment in the cities and towns the friars built some new though not particularly large chapels, such as those in Dublin and Drogheda. During the brief period of optimism before the Williamite wars large churches were built, such as those at Francis Street, Dublin, Athlone and Wexford.

During the Penal Laws a normal Franciscan residence was a small thatched cottage with another thatched building serving as a chapel nearby. In some cases mediaeval transept chapels were roofed over and used for this purpose, for instance Claregalway. The ruins of a small chapel built in the eighteenth century and used up to 1850 still survive at Meelick, where the remains of a two-storey residence dating to the second half of the eighteenth century also stand. A similar building at Aglish in Co. Waterford housed friars working as parish clergy. In the towns the friars lived in ordinary houses such as the large cottage still standing in Clonmel, or the cottage and small oratory whose outline can be traced in Thurles. The chapels of the seventeenth and eighteenth centuries were decorated with paintings and statues but few if any of these have survived. However, practically every modern friary has a collection of chalices and other altarplate dating to that period. Decoration on the early pieces is often minimal, consisting of a crude figure of the crucified Christ.

Chalices from the eighteenth century are more ornate and have the IHS monogram, often accompanied by a cross, and with vines around the base and angels heads on the stem.

## Modern Architecture

In the early nineteenth century thatched chapels were replaced by barn churches. Some modern friary churches incorporate elements from this phase but these earlier buildings have mostly been destroyed by later additions and rebuildings, as in Limerick and Cork where later churches have been built over demolished predecessors. The next phase was the extended barn type of church, of which there are two examples extant, Drogheda and Carrick-on-Suir. This type of structure belongs to the 1830s, and was characterized by a rectangular church with two small transepts. During this period work began on the churches in Dublin, Galway and Waterford, while the church in Multyfarnham was reopened. It is the only mediaeval church still used by the Franciscans, although part of Clonmel and possibly Wexford date to mediaeval times. A report in 1838 stated that practically all the friary churches had been rebuilt or updated within the previous decade.

With the exception of Killarney, built in their own tradition by Belgian friars in the 1860s and still unique among Irish churches, no new Franciscan buildings were constructed for fifty years. Limerick, Ennis and Clonmel were built in the 1880s, Ennis and Clonmel in the Gothic Revival style. During the first half of the twentieth century many of the existing churches were enlarged or re-decorated and the church in Dublin completed, but only two new churches were built, Athlone and Cork. Athlone is a good example of Hiberno-Romanesque, Cork is in the Hiberno-Byzantine style. The church at Rossnowlagh was built in the 1950s, the college chapel at Gormanston in the 1960s and the parish church at Ballywaltrim outside Bray in the 1980s. Each is typical of the architectural style of its decade. The churches have all been updated to accommodate the liturgical changes since Vatican II.

There is no unifying theme among contemporary Franciscan churches. They vary greatly in size and style, and many were considered innovative in their time. Several are decorated with works of art by leading artists, for example, Athlone Friary has stained glass from the Harry Clarke Studios and Dublin Craftworkers, and lunettes in *opus-sectile* outside by Ethel Mary Rhind and C. A. O'Brien, to which a cross by Muriel Brandt was later added. Common to the design of all the churches is the desire that these clean and well appointed houses of God should serve the needs of their congregations.

103

# GAZETTEER

# I

# FRANCISCAN SITES IN IRELAND

## ADARE (Co. Limerick)

Site at the far end of the golf course, or through the Dunraven Estate. Remains: church complete with tower and transept chapel; large sections of the convent and cloister; old gateway and some outbuildings. Notable Features: bas relief of St Francis in the cloister, traces of floral patterns on the top right tomb in the choir; at least two wooden statues exist, one of St Francis, the other of St Louis.

Begun in 1464 and dedicated to St Michael two years later, Adare friary was one of the first Observant foundations, and was built by order of Thomas FitzGerald, earl of Kildare. The friars remained until *c.* 1578. They returned in 1633 and remained, except for a brief period during the Cromwellian persecution, until the middle of the following century.

Caroline, Countess of Dunraven, *Memorials of Adare Manor* (Oxford 1865); Begley, J.: *Diocese of Limerick* (3 vols, Dublin 1906-38).

## ARAN (Inishmore, Co. Galway)

Site near St Eany's Round Tower in Killeany, at 'The Lodge'. Remains: nothing substantial, since the stones were used to build Arkin's Castle in 1587.

Begun in 1485 for the Conventual friars, Aran friary was suppressed after the arrival of Sir John Rawson in 1587. Efforts to restore it in the 1640s were unsuccessful.

## ARDFERT (Co. Kerry)

Site in fields a kilometre north-east of the village and the cathedral. Remains: the church and transept chapel are complete, as is the tower, which is situated in an unusual position at the west end of the church; a small section of the convent still stands, with the cloister. Notable feature: Sheela-na-gig on tower.

The friary was founded by Thomas FitzMaurice *c.* 1253. It became

105

*South elevation, Ardfert Friary, Co. Kerry*

an Observant Foundation in 1517. The tower was fortified as a barracks in 1584. The friars returned in 1613, after which they used the building intermittently until 1763. Local tradition names the last friar as Tim Sullivan.

Walsh, K., 'Franciscan Friaries in pre-Reformation Kerry', *JKAHS* ix (1976) 18-31.

## ARMAGH (City)
Site inside the gate of the Church of Ireland Primate's Palace, off the city by-pass.
Remains: three walls of the church, part of the transept chapel, all recently excavated.

There were friars in Armagh as early as 1241, but the permanent foundation there dates to 1263-4 during the episcopate of Archbishop Maol Padraig Ó Sgannail op. The friary was suppressed when the English took over the city in 1551. In 1561 Shane O'Neill burnt it to prevent it becoming an English stronghold· In 1565 it was raided and the friars publicly flogged. The house was again raided in 1587 and the remaining friars flogged and driven out. They found refuge in Brantry in Co. Tyrone and Creggan in Co. Armagh. In the seventeenth century the remnants of the community were united with Dungannon.

FitzMaurice, E. B., ofm, 'The Franciscans in Armagh', *UJA* (1900) 67-77; Lynn, C. J., 'Excavations in the Franciscan Friary Church, Armagh', *UJA* 38 (1975) 61-80.

## ASKEATON (Co. Limerick)
Site on the east bank of the river, north of the village.
Remains: church and transept chapel complete, but tower has fallen;
convent and cloisters complete, they are situated on the south side of
the church which is unusual; the refectory is a later addition; traces
of the boundary wall and outbuildings. Notable features: the bas
relief of St Francis in the north-east corner of the cloister, which
shows the stigmata; many masons' marks; the tomb of the unknown
pilgrim; bas relief of unknown bishop in the choir; excellent reader's
desk in the refectory; wooden statue exists.

Founded by Gearóid *File*, fourth earl of Desmond, before 1400, but
the present friary buildings date to slightly later. The community
became Observant in 1497 and was suppressed in 1579, when the
building was sacked by Nicholas Malby and several friars were
killed. Some managed to remain in the area and returned to the old
building in 1627. The friars remained active until 1740. Some friars
were acting as curates in Glin as late as 1766.

Westropp, T. J., 'Notes on Askeaton', *JRSAI* (1903) 32-9, 167-70;
Begley, J. *The Diocese of Limerick* (3 vols, Dublin 1906-38); MacLeod,
C., 'A Carved Oak Nursing Madonna from Askeaton, County
Limerick' in E. Rynne (ed.) *Figures from the Past* (Dublin 1987), 249-
57.

## ATHLONE (Co. Westmeath)
The mediaeval site was a hundred metres south of the abbey
graveyard. All later sites were in the vicinity of the present friary.
Remains: the stones of the mediaeval friary were used to build
Athlone bridge and to provide the foundation of the present church;
the ruins at Abbey Road are those of a church begun in 1687 and
which may never have been used.

The friary church in Athlone was consecrated in 1241. Charles de
Burgo was the principal founder. The building was badly damaged
by a malicious fire in 1398. The friary was destroyed in 1567 but the
friars remained in the town and adopted the Observant reform in
1587. They built a new house near the site of the old friary in 1626.
They also had a place of refuge at nearby Killinure, where Br
Micheál Ó Cléirigh spent some time in the late 1620s collecting and
copying mss. The friars were expelled from the town in 1651. At that
time the community consisted of eighteen friars. Some must have
remained in hiding as indicated by the death of Br John O'Claffey,
killed in 1653. The friars took over the present site early in the
eighteenth century and during the eighteenth and early nineteenth
centuries they worked as parish clergy. Work on the new friary began
in 1869 and a school, St Bonaventure's Academy, was opened in 107

1871. The foundation stone of the present Hiberno-Romanesque church was laid in 1930 Since 1975 a friar has been curate in the parish.

Grannell, F., ofm, *The Franciscans in Athlone* (Athlone 1978); McNamee, J. J., *History of the Diocese of Ardagh*, (Dublin 1954).

### BALLINABARNY (Co. Wicklow)
The site is near the Glen of Imaal.
There was a friary here for a number of years in the 1640s.

### BALLINASAGGART (Co. Longford)
The site is south-west of Edgeworthstown. There are no surviving buildings, only an outline remains.
The friary of St John the Baptist of Longford was founded as a Third Order Regular friary in the fifteenth century. The First Order received permission to take it over in 1635. The friary was plundered by the earl of Westmeath in 1651, but the friars had returned to the area by 1658. There were still four friars resident in 1801. The house ceased to exist after the death of Fr Thomas McCormick in 1811, although Fr Charles Kane did work as parish priest of Templemichael until his death in 1828.

McNamee, J. J., *History of the Diocese of Ardagh* (Dublin 1954).

### BALLYMOTE (Co. Sligo)
The site is near the present Catholic church.
Remains: almost complete church, with traces of the convent.
A Third Order friary, founded in 1442, it was taken over by the First Order *c.* 1643, and used by them for nearly a hundred years afterwards.

### BANTRY (Co. Cork)
The site was in the present abbey graveyard, where some of the stones belonging to the friary have been gathered together. There is one carved head among these.
Founded by an O'Sullivan or an O'Mahoney, Bantry friary became Observant in 1482 after twenty years as a Conventual site. The building was pulled down by Domhnall O'Sullivan Beare in 1599 to prevent the English from using it. Individual friars remained in the area, especially at Cape Clear, until the middle of the eighteenth century.

Bolster, E., *A History of the Diocese of Cork*, Vol. 1 (Shannon 1972), Vol. 2 (Cork 1982).

## BELFAST (Co. Antrim)

The site is the Church of St Joseph, Pilot Street, in the former docklands area.

After Bishop Cathal B. Daly was translated from Ardagh and Clonmacnois to Down and Connor in 1982, he invited the friars to the diocese. They took over an old church in a run-down part of the city and developed it as a Franciscan house. The first two friars moved in on 16 March 1984 and there is now a community of four; two priests and two brothers.

Heatley, F., *St Joseph's Centenary* 1872-1972; *Story of a Dockside Parish* (Belfast 1972).

## BONAMARGY (Co. Antrim)

The site is off the A2, beside Ballycastle Golf Club.

Remains: a small church, the transept chapel of which has been turned into the burial vault of the earls of Antrim; also parts of the convent and outhouses.

Founded for the Third Order Regular *c.* 1500, the friary was burned by the Irish and Scots in 1584 while it was being used by the English army. In 1626 it was taken over by the First Order and used as a base for the Scottish mission until 1647. The friars occasionally returned to the site afterwards, either with the aim of re-opening the Scottish mission, or in connection with parish work, which continued until the death of Fr Michael McMullin in 1789.

McKeown, L., 'Bonamargy . . . ', *Down & Connor Hist. Jn.*, iii (1930); Bigger, F. J. & Fennell, W. J., *The Ancient Franciscan Friary of Bonamargy*, *UJA* supplementary volume (1898).

## BRAY (Co. Wicklow)

The parish of St Fergal, Ballywaltrim, south of Bray.

The friars first considered opening a house in this area in 1873, but the plan was abandoned.

Following discussions with the diocesan authorities, it was agreed in May 1975 that the friars would take over a parish in the rapidly expanding area of Ballywaltrim. The parish was formally erected in May 1976. The church was dedicated to St Fergal by Archbishop Ryan on 21 December 1980, by which time a new presbytery-cum-friary was already in operation nearby. The increasing size of the parish has led to the acquisition of a second house for friars working in local schools.

Millett, B., ofm, 'The Franciscans in County Wicklow', *Arch. Fran. Hist.*, lxxvii (1984).

*East window, Buttevant Friary, Co. Cork*

## BUTTEVANT (Co. Cork)

The site is on the main street beside the present Catholic church.
Remains: the church and transept are complete, but the tower has
fallen; many stones belonging to the cloister arcade are stored in the
upper vault under the choir; there are carved stones in the lower
vault; many of the windows in the church have been rebuilt.

Dedicated to St Thomas à Becket, the friary was founded by the de
Barry family, before 1276, possibly by 1251. The de Barrys also
protected the friars following the Reformation, and the friars

remained in the area until the Cromwellian period. They returned after the Restoration, and there were at least two of them in residence during the eighteenth century. By 1800 only one old friar remained. In 1815 the friar described as guardian of Buttevant was living and working in Cork.

De Barra, G., 'Buttevant . . . ' in J. O'Callaghan (ed.) *Franciscan Cork* (Cork 1953).

## CARRICKBEG (Co. Waterford)
The remains of the old friary have been incorporated into the present parish church across the road from the present friary.Notable features: the unusual tower, riding on the church wall, and the carved figures around the church door; folk-art St Francis in friary.

According to the *Annals* of Friar John Clyn, its first superior, the friary was founded in 1336 by James Butler, earl of Ormond. It was an early victim of the Suppression and was vacant for nearly a hundred years until the friars returned in 1644. Having been expelled by the Cromwellians, they returned again in 1669. They built a thatched house, and later a thatched chapel, in the grounds of the present friary. Following an 'accident' (when local fishermen pulled off the thatched roof and later pretended a storm caused the damage) a new church was built in 1822 and extended in 1839-49. The convent was added in 1896.

Crowley, W., ofm., *The Story of the Franciscan Church and Friary at Carrickbeg*, (Carrick-on-Suir 1978).

## CARRICKFERGUS (Co. Antrim)
The site is off Joymount Street. There are no remains, but the area was excavated in 1976-7.

An early Franciscan foundation, it received a royal grant in 1248. The Observant reform was introduced from Donegal in 1497. Suppressed early, it was used as a munitions store until it was re-built as Joymount House by Sir Arthur Chichester in 1618. After 1626 the friars made several attempts to return to the area, but were unsuccessful. Occasional parish work was carried on there by the friars in the eighteenth century.

McKeown, L., 'Carrickfergus . . . ' *Down & Connor Hist. Jn.*, iii (1930).

## CASHEL (Co. Tipperary)
The present Catholic parish church is on the site of the mediaeval friary.

Remains: while nothing remains of the buildings, some pieces of cut 111 stone and some carvings are kept in the Presentation Convent graveyard; a sarcophagus is used as a font in the parish church. Notable features: four tomb slabs, a knight and three ladies, have been inserted into the walls around the Church of Ireland cathedral.

'Hacket's Abbey' was founded by Lord William Hacket *c.*1265. It later became the principal house of one of the custodies of the Irish Franciscan province. It was suppressed in 1538, when Archbishop Edward Butler took possession of it, and finally abandoned by the friars in 1550. The friars returned to Cashel in 1618, but left after the sacking of the town by Lord Inchiquin in 1647. They were again present in 1658 and remained until the eighteenth century. For later history, see under Thurles.

Conlan, P., ofm., 'The Franciscan House in Thurles', *NMAJ*, xix (1977), 43-9.

## CASTLEDERMOT (Co. Kildare)

The site is outside the town on the Carlow road.

Remains: the church is complete with a large transept chapel and an unusual tower; there are three small side-chapels within the transept chapel.

Founded before 1247, Castledermot friary was given a substantial building grant by Thomas, lord of Ossory in 1302. Situated on the

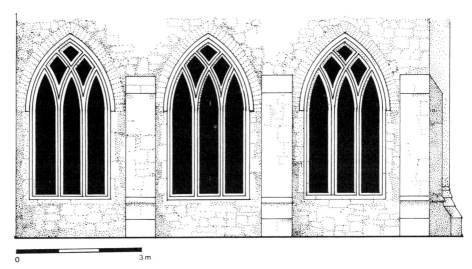

0          3 m

         *Aisle windows, Castledermot Friary, Co. Kildare*

edge of the Pale, it was plundered by Edward Bruce in 1317. It was still a Conventual house when suppressed in 1540. The Observant friars returned to the area in 1639 but were expelled by the Cromwellians. They came back again in 1661 and maintained a presence until the middle of the eighteenth century.

Comerford, M., 'The Friary in Castledermot', *JKAS*, i (1895).

## CASTLELYONS (Co. Cork)
The remains here are of a Carmelite friary, founded in 1307. However, there was a Franciscan residence in the area in the early eighteenth century, but the site has not been identified.

## CAVAN (town)
The site was that of the present graveyard in Abbey Street.
Remains: the tower is complete, but in a much-altered condition.

The town of Cavan grew up around the friary founded, according to tradition, by Giolla-Íosa O'Reilly, lord of Breffny, *c.* 1300. In 1451 the friary was burnt through the carelessness of a drunken friar. It was again burnt by the English in 1468. The Observant reform was introduced in the early sixteenth century. Many of the community were drowned in a boating accident in 1516. Despite the Suppression, the friars remained until 1608. They returned in 1616, and later acted as parish clergy. There were seven Franciscans working in the area in 1800, and two in 1820, of whom the last died in 1826.

Mooney, C., ofm, 'Some Cavan Franciscans', *Breifne*, i (1958-61) 17-27.

## CLANE (Co. Kildare)
The site is in the graveyard on the Naas road, to the south-east of the village.
Remains: large sections of the church and transept walls. Notable features: damaged effigy of a knight.

The effigy is said to be that of Gerald FitzMaurice FitzGerald, who is reputed to have founded the friary in 1258. Having undergone major re-building in 1433, the friary was suppressed in 1540 and stone from it was used to repair MaynoothCastle. The friars returned briefly to the area in the late 1640s.

Comerford, M., *Collections Relating to the Dioceses Kildare and Leighlinn* (3 vols, Dublin 1884-6).

## CLAREGALWAY (Co. Galway)
The site is to the west of the village, on the main Galway-Tuam road.   113

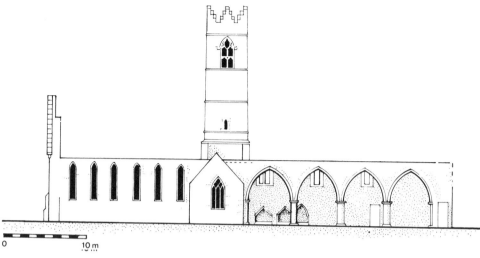

*North elevation, Claregalway Friary, Co. Galway*

Remains: the church, tower, large sections of the transept and aisle are almost complete; a large part of the convent still stands, on the south side of the church, which is unusual; there are traces of outbuildings and of the original gateway into the friary.

John de Cogan, who also founded the Carthusian house at Kinalehin (see below), founded the friary of Claregalway *c.* 1250. One of the largest friaries in the country, it remained Conventual until the Suppression. The friars were driven out by Sir Richard Bingham in 1589. Attempts were made to restore the friary after 1641. The friars were again expelled by the Cromwellians, but returned after the Restoration. There was a community of five living in the old friary in 1766, and four in 1801. Reduced to two by 1838, Fr John Francis withdrew to Galway in 1847 but continued to visit the site and say mass there until his death in 1858, after which the site was abandoned.

Mitchell, J., 'An Account of the Franciscan Friary and the Parish Churches at Claregalway during the Last Two Hundred and Fifty Years', *JGAHS*, 37 (1979-80) 5-34.

## CLONKEENKERRILL (Co. Galway)

The site is in an isolated graveyard about eight kilometres north of Attymon.

Remains: most of the church and transept chapel.

*C.* 1435, the bishop of Clonfert gave permission to two brothers, David and John Mulkerrill, to convert the old parish church into a Third Order friary. In 1453 permission was obtained to change to the

First Order. The friary was still occupied in 1618, but was abandoned soon afterwards.

## CLONMEL (Co. Tipperary)

The mediaeval site was that of the present friary church.

Remains: the tower and part of the choir wall are incorporated into the present church. Notable features: the tomb(1533) of the Butlers of Cahir; other sculptures include an early tradesman's tomb-stone and a stone baptismal font.

Founded in 1269, probably by Sir Otho de Grandison, the friary became Observant in 1536, four years before it was suppressed. The friars remained in the town and built a new house in 1616. After the Restoration they lived in Irishtown. During the eighteenth century they helped in parish work. Having obtained the old friary church once again, they re-opened it in 1828. They ran a school from 1873 to 1881. The present church was built, in what the architect believed was Early English style, and formally opened in 1886. The friary residence was added in 1891-2 and a small St Anthony Chapel built in 1959.

Burke, W. P., *History of Clonmel* (Waterford 1907); Gaynor, B., ofm, *Franciscan Church, Clonmel* (Clonmel 1986); Conlan, P., ofm, 'Clonmel Friary', *The Nationalist*, March-April 1974.

## CORK (City)

There are no remains of the mediaeval friary at the site on the North Mall.

The friary was founded before 1230 by Dermot McCarthy. It adopted the Observant reform *c.* 1500 and was suppressed in 1540. The friars remained in the city and there was a community of nine in their place of refuge in 1615. After the Restoration, the friars lived in a thatched cottage in Shandon and worked openly until the Penal period, during which they were forced to go into hiding, finally settling in the present Broad Lane area *c.* 1759. A new friary was opened in 1813, following which the Franciscan novitiate was transferred to Cork for a number of years. A dispute between the friars and the bishop of Cork, and fears that the religious Orders in Ireland were about to be suppressed, delayed the building of a new church, which was not opened until 1829. A student hostel called St Anthony's Hall was opened in 1909 but closed in 1912 after objections within the Order. By 1881 both friary and church were considered unsafe, but it was not until 14 July 1953 that the present church was opened and blessed, soon to be followed by the new friary in October 1958 and St Anthony's Shrine in April 1960.

Egan, B., ofm, *The Friars of Broad Lane* (Cork 1977); Egan, B., ofm, 'The Friars Minor and the Honan Hostel . . .', *Arch. Fran. Hist.*, lxxiii (1980); O'Callaghan, J., ofm, (ed.): *Franciscan Cork* (Cork 1953).

## COURTOWN (Co. Meath)

No trace of the site remains.

When the friary in Trim was threatened with closure *c.* 1700, the friars became involved in parish work in an area north of the town and also in the Navan area. From a house of refuge at Courtown, they served the parishes of Bective, Clonmaduff, Courtown, Kilcooley, Moymet, Rataine and Tullaghenoge. They also worked for some time in the parishes of Donaghmore, Donaghpatrick, Kilberry and Loghan. In 1801 there was a community of three at Courtown, and a parish priest and six curates working in the area. Courtown officially closed following the death of Fr Patrick Ryan in 1826.

Cogan, A., *The Diocese of Meath* (3 vols, Dublin 1862-70); Callery, P., 'The Grey Friars of Trim', *IER* (1913), 473-90.

## CURRAHEEN (Aglish, Co. Waterford)

The last official residence of the friars, a two-storey house, still stands.

Friars from Youghal fled across the river into Co. Waterford in the seventeenth century, but they retained the privileged title of Youghal. In the early eighteenth century the friars transferred the Youghal foundation to Curraheen and served in the church at Aglish. The surviving residence was built *c.* 1845. The last friar of Youghal, Fr P. D. Lonergan, died at Curraheen in 1862.

Power, P., *Waterford and Lismore Dioceses* (Dublin 1937).

## DERRY (City)

There is evidence for a small Franciscan residence in Derry in the late seventeenth century and a strong local tradition of a Franciscan presence in the Waterside and Ardmore areas. The only friar associated with the city was Fr Francis Gallagher, who taught in the seminary there before his death in 1806.

Faulkner, A., ofm, 'Franciscans of Derry and Inishowen', *Don. Ann.* (1982), 3-17.

## DERRYNAFLAN (Co. Tipperary)

There are remains of a mediaeval church on an island in the bog of Lurgoe, site of the discovery of altar plate in 1980.

This name appears in official documents from 1676 to 1724. The actual identification of the site is doubtful, but this island in the middle of a bog seems a likely place due to its associations with Cashel.

O'Callaghan, J., ofm, (ed.) *Franciscan Cork* (Cork 1953), 76.

## DONEGAL (town)

The site is in a graveyard near the shore of Donegal bay.
Remains: parts of the choir, transept chapel and cloisters.

Donegal friary was a late foundation. It was founded by Nuala O'Connor, her son the first Red Hugh O'Donnell, and his wife Nuala O'Brien, for the Observant friars in 1473-4. It was damaged by an accidental fire in 1536. It escaped suppression until raided by the English in 1588, who then occupied it as a fort. They were expelled by Red Hugh O'Donnell in 1592. His brother-in-law, Niall Garbh, seized it for the English again in 1601. On the morning of 20 September 1601 the building was severely damaged when the gun-powder stored in it exploded. Efforts to re-build it were abandoned after the Flight of the Earls. The friars continued to live in a house of refuge near the river Drowes, where much of the work on the *Annals of the Four Masters* was carried out. Individual friars worked in Donegal until the mid-nineteenth century. The late Cardinal Logue, who was born in 1840, claimed that he had been baptised by a wandering friar in south Donegal!

O'Donnell, T., ofm (ed.), *Franciscan Donegal* (Rossnowlagh 1952).

## DONNYBROOK (Co. Dublin)

Site at Broc House, Nutley Lane.

When UCD was transferred from Earlsfort Terrace to Belfield the Franciscans decided to open a hostel there. It was hoped that the hostel, which was opened in 1971 would also be a suitable venue for international conferences. The venture was not a success. The student section closed in 1976 and the hotel function in 1977. It has been retained as a residence for friars engaged in teaching and other work. After 1980 the pastoral year for the newly ordained was replaced by a diaconate year based at Broc House. A friar now works as a curate in the parish.

## DOWNPATRICK (town)

No remains of the original structure survive, the presumed site is that of the courthouse.

Downpatrick was one of the two major towns in the earldom of  117

Ulster. The earl, Hugh de Lacy, founded the friary *c*. 1235. It was burned by Bruce in 1316. It remained a Conventual house until the Reformation. The friars remained in the town until three were killed by an English force in 1575. Observant friars returned to the town in 1627 and remained until the Cromwellian period. For later history, see under Dromore.

## DROGHEDA (Co. Louth)

Nothing remains of the early friary, which was situated between the Laurence Gate and the river.

Drogheda friary was founded *c*. 1240, but the exact details are uncertain. In 1330 the building was badly damaged by flooding, and, in 1349 twenty-five members of the community died during the Black Death. The community did not become Observant until 1506. Suppressed in 1540, it was abandoned about five years later. Some friars continued to visit the city, since one was arrested for saying mass there in 1607, but a formal community was not re-established until 1610. During the seventeenth and eighteenth centuries the friars came and went as circumstances permitted. In 1798 they purchased an old store for conversion into a chapel, but work could not begin until 1829. The first mass was celebrated there on 22 August 1830. Extensions were undertaken in 1835 and again in 1842. Drogheda friary became a favoured house within the Irish province, and the novitiate was there from 1860 to 1877. There is also evidence for a friary school at Drogheda.

The 'Brown', or reform, friars took over in 1923. By 1942 it was clear that the structural condition of both church and friary was unsatisfactory. The friary is currently undergoing substantial rebuilding. On 1 October 1980 the friars took over the parish of Mell, with Fr Jude O'Riordan as parish priest. Initially they used the old chapel at Mell, though it was envisaged that a new church and presbytery would be built. The anticipated residential development has not taken place and construction plans have been postponed.

Conlan, P., ofm, *The Franciscans in Drogheda* (Drogheda 1987).

## DROMAHAIR (Creevelea Friary, Co. Leitrim)

The friary of Creevelea is in a graveyard in a wooded area a kilometre west of Dromahair village.

Remains: a church with transept chapel and tower (altered); large sections of the convent and cloister. Notable features: a large quantity of good stone-work; the flamboyant east and west windows in the church; reliefs on the mullions of the east window; animal motifs under the tower; especially two bas-reliefs of St Francis on the side of a pillar in the cloister, one of St Francis preaching to the birds, the other of St Francis with the stigmata.

Founded in 1508 for Observant friars from Donegal by Margaret O'Brien and her husband, Eoghan O'Rourke, it was the last pre-Reformation Franciscan foundation in Ireland. Before being completed, the buildings were badly damaged by an accidental fire in 1536. It was partially restored by Brian Ballagh O'Rourke. In 1590 it was used as a barracks by English forces under Sir Richard Bingham. It was 1618 before the friars were again able to set up a permanent residence. They were forced to flee during Cromwellian times, but returned after the Restoration, when they became involved in parish work in the area. The last friar of Dromahair was Fr Peter Magauran, who died in 1837.

McNamee, J. J., *History of the Diocese of Ardagh* (Dublin 1954).

## DROMORE (Co. Down)

The exact site is uncertain and there are no surviving remains.

A residence was set up in Dromore following the provincial chapter of 1637 to relieve pressure on the friars of Downpatrick. During the eighteenth century the friars continued to work in the area. They set up a school at Drumnacoile, which was eventually handed over to lay teachers. Only one priest was still alive in 1796, having spent a life-time serving the local chapel. He died before 1800.

O'Laverty, J., *An Historical Account of the Diocese of Down and Connor* (5 vols, Dublin 1876-95).

## DUBLIN (City)

The site of the mediaeval friary was that of the Catholic church in Francis Street. There are no remains and all later sites were in the Cook Street area.

A group of friars travelled to Dublin shortly after the initial landing at Youghal and established a house there *c.* 1230. The early history of the Dublin friary is obscure. Some authorities suggest the friars tried a number of sites before settling in the modern Francis Street. Henry III was a notable benefactor, if not the actual founder. At least twenty-three friars died there during the Black Death. The Observant reform was introduced *c.* 1521. It was an early target for suppression, but the community were able to continue in existence until 1543.

While individual friars may have continued to live in the city, it was not until 1615 that a community returned and took up residence in Cook Street. Following a raid on 26 December 1629 they were forced to find another house in the same area. Expelled by the Cromwellians, the friars returned after the Restoration and tried to resume residence at their old site in Francis Street. The chapel they erected there served as the pro-Cathedral of Dublin until it was replaced by the present church of St Nicholas in 1834.

The friars also returned to Cook Street, where their church was in such a bad state of repair that it collapsed. A new chapel was opened in 1749, behind the parish church of St Michael. In 1766 there were nine friars in the community, and three more engaged in parish work in other parts of the city. By this time the friars had obtained a small house on Merchant's Quay. To disguise the chapel, the entrance was through the Adam and Eve Inn, thus the popular name of the present church and friary.

The old church of St Michael was purchased in 1815. The foundation stone of a new church and friary was laid on 16 April 1834. The architect was Patrick Byrne, whose original plan was never fully carried out as the building took over a century to complete and the church was not consecrated until 29 April 1939, by which time apse, dome, aisles, facade and shrines had been added to the original design. The friary itself was modernized and extended in 1946-8. As part of the re-organization of the central Dublin parishes, the Church of the Immaculate Conception, Merchant's Quay, to use the official title, became parish church of a new parish in 1974.

Cleary, G., ofm, *The Friars Minor in Dublin 1233-1939* (Dublin 1939); McClean, L., ofm (ed.), *Adam and Eve, Church of the Immaculate Conception* (2nd ed., Dublin 1962).

## DUNDALK (Co. Louth)

The site is in Seatown, at the corner of Castle Street and Mill Street. Remains: the tower, unusual in that it stood at the end of the aisle. Notable feature: a baptismal font in St Nicholas church is reputed to have come from the friary.

The friary was founded before 1246 by the de Verdon family. Twenty-three friars were killed when it was burned by Bruce in 1315. It was still a Conventual house when it was seized in 1539 by order of Sir Leonard Grey. The friars went to live in a small cottage nearby. They adopted the observant reform in 1556, and were driven out in 1563. The friars returned in 1626, when they became engaged in a dispute with the Carmelites over priorities. A similar dispute after the Restoration, this time with the Dominicans, involved the primate, St Oliver Plunkett. Although there was a community of seven in 1731, the friars left the town in the following year. They continued to work in neighbouring country parishes, especially at Creggan in south Armagh, where one of them was still working as a curate in 1801.

O'Sullivan, H., 'The Franciscans in Dundalk', *Sean. Ardmh.* (1960-1), 33-71.

## DUNGANNON (Co. Tyrone)

There are traces of a house and church near the top of Drumbeam Hill.

In 1687, the existing fifteenth-century Third Order foundation at Dungannon was re-constituted as a First Order house, to relieve pressure on Armagh. Eventually the two communities were united into one and settled near Donaghmore where there were seven friars in 1766. The friars became involved in parish work and the last friar, Fr Francis O'Neill, died in 1816-7 while acting as parish priest in the area.

Mooney, C., ofm, 'The Franciscan First Order Friary at Dungannon', in *Sean. Admh.* (1955), 72-93.

## ELPHIN (Co. Roscommon)

The site was at the eastern end of the village, but there are no significant remains.

Cornelius, bishop of Elphin, granted the parish church of St Patrick to the friars before 1450. The early Irish monastery, an alleged Patrician site, had been taken over by the Canons Regular of St Augustine *c.* 1140, but the church had ceased to be the cathedral of the diocese in 1244, and the site had fallen into disuse by 1440. The friars were expelled by the Protestant bishop in 1563. He had the building knocked and built a house with the stone. Observant friars returned in 1632. Expelled by the Cromwellians, the friars shipped some of their valuables to Louvain in 1654! They returned again in 1658 and there was a community of nine in 1766. The second last friar in the community went to Rome in 1787, leaving one old bed-ridden friar behind. Soon after, the parish priest of Castlereagh paid for the education of a number of friars from the area in the hope of restoring Elphin friary. One of these, Fr Edward Garraghan, who was minister provincial in 1815-9, worked near Elphin for most of his life until he died in 1835, as parish priest of Kilcorkey.

Giblin, C., ofm, 'The Franciscans in Elphin', Roscommon HAST 2 (1988), 23-9.

## ENNIS (Co. Clare)

The old friary is situated around the corner from the present one.

Remains: church, tower and transept chapel are complete, as are the east range and parts of the cloister. Notable features: there is a considerable amount of cut stone and some notable bas-reliefs including the reconstructed MacMahon tomb, St Francis with the stigmata, and a small *Ecce Homo*.

Donnach O'Brien founded Ennis friary on an island near his castle and the town grew up around both. The construction of the friary had begun before the death of Donnach in 1242. However, it was substantially re-built by Turlough Mór O'Brien towards the end of the thirteenth century. Later Ennis friary became a famous centre of learning. It adopted the Observant reform in the mid-sixteenth century. The house was suppressed in 1543, but the community remained until 1575. Individual friars still remained, such as 'The Mad Friar', Fr Dermot O'Brien, who was certified insane so that he could live within the town *c.* 1617. A small community was established in the area in 1627. During the Cromwellian period the friars seem to have had places of refuge at Doolough Lake and Inagh. Following the Decree for the Expulsion of Religious, at least four friars registered as parish clergy, while others continued to live in the vicinity. By 1800 they were living as a community in Lysaght's Lane, and they opened a new chapel and friary at Bow Lane on 12 December 1830. Following a threat by the provincial in 1853 that he would close Ennis friary unless conditions were improved, the present site at Willow Bank House was obtained and the first mass was celebrated in the new church there on 1 January 1856. Twenty years later this building was replaced by the present church, which was officially opened on 11 June 1892 although it had been in use since 1886. Ennis became the official novitiate of the Irish province from 1876 to 1902. The old mediaeval friary was returned to the friars as an ecumenical gesture by the Church of Ireland in 1969.

Conlan, P., ofm, *Franciscan Ennis* (Ennis 1984); Hunt, J., 'The Influence of Alabaster Carvings on Mediaeval Sculpture in Ennis Friary', *NMAJ*, xviii (1975), 35-9.

## ENNISCORTHY (Co. Wexford)

The site was off the present Abbey Square.
Remains: most of the stones were used to build the Catholic cathedral in the nineteenth century; an old doorway belonging to the friary is still preserved at Lett's Brewery.

Founded in 1460, possibly for the Observants, by Donal Reagh Cavanagh, little is known of the history of Enniscorthy friary before its suppression in 1540. The friars remained on and three of them were killed when the friary was plundered by Sir Henry Wallop in

1582. The rest of the community had dispersed by the end of the century. The friars returned between 1642 and 1650, and again after 1661. By 1688 they were involved in parish work. Government reports of 1731 indicate that there was no longer a community of friars in the area.

Grattan Flood, W. H., *History of the Diocese of Ferns* (Waterford 1916); Grannell, F., ofm, *The Franciscans in Wexford* (Wexford 1975).

## GALBALLY (Moor Abbey, Co. Tipperary)
The site is about two kilometres to the east of the village.
Remains: the church and tower are complete, but nothing remains of the convent.

Galbally was a late Conventual foundation, begun in 1471. After its suppression in 1540 it was granted to John, brother of the earl of Desmond, who allowed the friars to remain. Sir Humphrey Gilbert burned the building in 1569, and Sir Henry Sidney also burned it in 1570. The friars did not return until 1645. Expelled by the Cromwellians, they were back in 1658 and remained, except for a short break during 1680-4, until 1748. Following a dispute with Fr James Butler, vicar general of Cashel diocese, the friars of Galbally withdrew across the mountains to Mitchelstown, where the last friar of Galbally community died, *c.* 1804.

## GALWAY ABBEY (City)
The mediaeval friary was on St Stephen's Island, where the courthouse now stands.
Remains: there are no substantial remains of the buildings, but an interesting collection of mediaeval tombstones can be seen in the present friary garden.

William de Burgo founded the Franciscan friary in Galway in 1296. After 1438 it housed a school for higher theological studies. In the early fifteenth century both Conventuals and Observants lived in Galway friary and disputed its affiliation. The co-operation of the local officials enabled the friars to escape suppression and to remain until 1583, when they were expelled. On their return in 1612 they probably settled on the present site, but were again expelled by the Cromwellians. They returned in 1660 and were able to maintain a community there throughout the eighteenth century (four in 1724, thirteen in 1766, six in 1801). Work on a new church began in 1781, but the present building was not finished until *c.* 1836, and not consecrated until 1849. The friary in its present form dates from 1820. The church is reputed to be the first in Ireland which was dedicated to the Immaculate Conception. The area around the 123

'Abbey' became the first Franciscan parish in modern Ireland in 1971.

Mac Donncha, F., ofm, *The Abbey of St Francis, Galway* (Galway 1971).

## GALWAY COLLEGE (City)

The rapid expansion of the Irish Franciscan province in the 1920s necessitated the making of new arrangements for the education of students. It was decided that they would attend UCG from 1932 on. The foundation stone of a permanent student house, the present St Anthony's College, was laid on 25 April 1933. A new wing was added in 1941 to allow for the 'student explosion' caused by the closure of the college in Louvain and the impossibility of sending new students to Rome during the Second World War. Due to problems associated with the points system and choice of courses, a transfer of students to UCD began in 1987.

## GOLEEN (Co. Cork)

This site is the probable location of the friary of Gahannyh.

Little is known about this foundation. It was under repair by Friar Donald O'Scully in 1442 when Pope Eugenius IV granted an indulgence to assist the work.

O'Callaghan, J., ofm (ed.), *Franciscan Cork* (Cork 1953), 84.

## GOREY (Co. Wexford)

There are no remains of the friars' residence, but the nuns' convent still stands.

The Ram family invited the Franciscan Sisters of Perpetual Adoration to settle in Gorey and some Belgian Franciscans were asked to join the community as chaplains. Permission was given for the foundation on 11 September 1858. The Belgian friars hoped to reform the Irish Franciscans by their example. When the bishop would not grant them the privilege of having a public church, the Belgians moved to Killarney on 9 July 1860.

Conlan, P., ofm, 'The Franciscan Friary, Killarney 1860-1902', *JKAHS*, x (1977), 77-110.

## GORMANSTON (Co. Meath)

Gormanston Castle, the ancestral home of the Preston family, was purchased by the Irish friars in 1947. The Irish Franciscans links with the Preston family went back to the seventeenth century, when Irish friars were chaplains to the regiment of Preston in Flanders.

After some years it was decided to move the seraphic college from Multyfarnham and build a new school at Gormanston. The first pupils arrived on 10 September 1954, but the transfer was not completed until September 1956. A formal opening by the bishop of Meath, Dr Kyne, in the presence of Cardinal d'Alton, who gave the oration, took place on the memorial day of Fr Luke Wadding, 18 November 1956. It had been intended to dedicate the college to his memory but instead it was dedicated to the Immaculate Conception. Construction of the school was finished in September 1957, and of the chapel in 1960. A special language laboratory was opened in 1965. The school now caters for about four hundred and forty boarders and a hundred day students.

Conlan, P., ofm, 'Gormanston 1947-54', *Fran. Coll. Ann.* (Gormanston 1985-6).

### JAMESTOWN (Co. Leitrim)

The remains of a small church associated with the friars still stand beside the river.

Jamestown was a plantation town, so it is unlikely that the friars took up residence there until after its capture by the Irish in 1642. The friars were certainly there by 1644. In August 1650 the friary was the site of a national synod which condemned Ormond and his political associates. It would seem that Fr Bernard Egan continued to work in the area during the Cromwellian period. He later became minister provincial and held the chapters of 1660 and 1661 there. The friars maintained strong links with the area during the eighteenth century. As late as 1801 there was a community of four, probably in Drumreilly Lower. The last friar of Jamestown, Fr Anthony Dunne, died *c.* 1825. The Franciscan Brothers of the Third Order Regular had a school there until *c.* 1835.

Mooney, C., ofm, 'The Franciscan Friary of Jamestown' *JACAS*, (1946), 3-25; Mac Namee, J. J., *History of the Diocese of Ardagh* (Dublin 1954).

### KILCONNELL (Co. Galway)

The site is on the northern side of the village.

Remains: the church is complete, with tower and transept chapel; the east range of the convent and some sections of the cloister remain. Notable features: two excellent flamboyant tombs in the nave; several carvings, in particular an owl, under the tower; part of a wooden statue of Our Lady also exists.

Kilconnell friary was founded by William O'Kelly, lord of Uí    125

Máine, in 1414. The Observant reform was introduced before 1464. The friary seems to have escaped suppression until the Cromwellian period, although the friars were forced to abandon the building for short periods. According to local tradition they finally departed before the battle of Aughrim in 1691, but this is rather unlikely. In fact they were working in the area during most of the eighteenth century – there were two at Monabraithre in 1709, ten in 1766. Some of these friars ministered as diocesan clergy. By 1801 the last friar had left: a secular parish priest was appointed in 1799.

Bigger, F. J., 'The Franciscan Friary of Kilconnell', *JGAHS* (1900-1).

## KILCREA (Co. Cork)

The site is near Farran on the Cork to Bantry road.

Remains: both church and convent are almost complete, including a well-preserved scriptorium, although some of the cut stone has been removed; a small ivory crucifix from Kilcrea is kept in Cork friary.

One of the early Observant foundations, Kilcrea, was founded by Cormac Mac Carthy, lord of Muskerry, in 1465. The house was protected from suppression by the Mac Carthys and the friars were able to remain in residence until a raid by the English forces in 1584, when two soldiers were killed in a fight over the spoils. When a

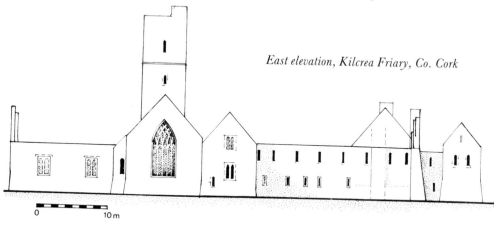

*East elevation, Kilcrea Friary, Co. Cork*

permanent garrison was established in Kilcrea Castle (1599), the friars had to withdraw, but they had returned by 1603 and were finally expelled in 1644. The building was fortified and used as a barracks by Cromwellian forces in the 1650s. The friars continued to work in the area during the eighteenth century. In 1731 the Protestant bishop of Cork complained of the friars who 'creep into the houses of the weak and ignorant people, confirming the Papists in their errors'. By 1776 the remaining friars had withdrawn to Cork city, from where they continued to do occasional work in the Kilcrea region until *c.* 1815. One friar lived in Kilcrea from 1778 to 1787.

Walsh, T. J., 'The Friary of Kilcrea', in *Franciscan Cork* (Cork 1953); O Gibeallāin, A., ofm., 'The Franciscan Friary of Kilcrea' in *Kilcrea Friary* 1465-1965 (Cork 1966).

## KILCULLEN (Co. Kildare)

The site is that of the New Abbey graveyard, about two kilometres south of the village.
Remains: most of the stone was removed during the building of New Abbey House; part of the old friary was converted into a Catholic chapel in Penal times; low walls mark the outline of this building, which was knocked down about a century ago; a tomb of the founder of the friary, Sir Roland Fitz Eustace, 1st Baron Portlester (d. 1496) and his wife, Margaret Jennico, is in the graveyard; there is another in St Audoen's Church (C of I), Dublin.

Founded in 1486 for the Observants, the friary of Kilcullen was officially suppressed in 1539. The friars remained in residence until 1547 and except for a short period in the 1640s, did not try to take up residence in the area again.

## KILDARE (town)

The site is Grey Abbey graveyard, a little to the south of the town.
Remains: parts of the walls of the choir and nave.

The traditional burial place of the earls of Kildare, the friary was founded by Gerald FitzMaurice *c.* 1254-60. With the help of Joan de Burgo, large scale expansion of the buildings took place *c.* 1350. The Observant reform was introduced in 1520. The friary was suppressed in 1539. The buildings were partially destroyed during a raid by the O'Connors in the following year, and were finally abandoned in 1547. The friars returned to the area in 1621 and continued to work there for about a hundred and fifty years, except during the Cromwellian period. In 1698 there were nine regulars (not all Franciscans) in the county, while the provincial was in hiding there in 1712. In 1731 there was no community but wandering preachers were active in the area.

Comerford, M., *Collections Relating to the Dioceses of Kildare and Leighlin* (3 vols, Dublin 1884-6).

## KILKENNY (City)

The site is in the grounds of the Smithwicks brewery: the sacristy has    127 been restored as an oratory.

Remains: only the tower and choir still stand; excavation revealed that the original building was almost identical with Castledermot friary. Notable features: there is a good sedelia in the choir; excellent finials under the tower, and a respond nearby.

Founded by the Marshall family *c.* 1232, Kilkenny friary underwent large-scale expansion and re-building early in the fourteenth century. The community remained Conventual until its suppression in 1540. The friars were expelled from the city in 1550, but returned from 1553 to 1559. The Observant friars came to Kilkenny in 1612. When Fr John Dalton ofm was caught and hanged by the Cromwellians in August 1653, he was the last priest in the city. The friars returned again after the Restoration. They became involved in parish work during the eighteenth century and there were still three friars working in the diocese of Ossory in 1801. The last friar of Kilkenny, Fr Philip Forrestall, died in 1829 after many years of parish work.

Carrigan, W., *The History and Antiquities of the Diocese of Ossory*, Vol. ii (Dublin 1905); Conlan, P., ofm, 'St Francis Abbey, Kilkenny', *OKR* (1975), 80-4.


## KILLARNEY (Co. Kerry)

The design of the building is based on Muckross friary. Notable feature: the Flemish-style woodwork in the church.

When the Belgian friars left Gorey in 1860, they settled in Killarney at the invitation of the bishop of Kerry, Dr Moriarty. The Belgians were hoping to establish a friary which would be an example for the Irish Franciscans. The bishop was looking for a re-incarnation of the spirit of Muckross. The site chosen was Martyrs' Hill, where Fr Cornelius MacCarthy had been put to death in 1652 and Fr Thaddeus Moriarty in 1653. The foundation stone of the new church was laid on 17 March 1864. Killarney became part of the newly erected English Franciscan custody in 1887, and of the new English province in 1891, when it was also serving as the English novitiate. Surplus to requirements, it was sold to the Irish province in 1902 and became the novitiate, which it has remained ever since.

Conlan, P., ofm, 'Franciscan Friary, Killarney, 1860-1902' *JKAHS*, x (1977) 79-110; Younge, P., ofm, *The Franciscan Friary* (Killarney 1984).


## KILLEENAGALLIVE (Co. Tipperary)

There are no remains on the site, which is on the Tipperary-Limerick border, near Emly.

This friary was founded for the Third Order by King Edward IV before 1461. It may have been used by the First Order from 1615 to 1625 and again from 1676 to 1690.

## KILLEIGH (Co. Offaly)

One wall of the church remains, outside the village on the Tullamore road.

The friary was founded in 1293, possibly by O'Conor Fallighe. It remained a Conventual house until the seventeenth century. It was plundered by Lord Grey in 1537-8. A community of friars remained in residence until *c.* 1580. Individual friars continued to live in the area until the Observants re-established a community in 1632. While in hiding during the Cromwellian period, the guardian of Killeigh was appointed vicar provincial, but he died before the information reached him. The community re-emerged in 1658. By the following century they had become involved in parish work. In 1770-80 two friars living at Cully tried to revive the friary. Fr John Egan died as parish priest of Eglish in 1807. Fr J. J. Donovan worked in the Killurin area *c.* 1821, trying to found a Franciscan school. He was a member of the Athlone community between 1825 and 1847, but was always interested in reviving an Offaly friary.

Shaw, A. L., *The Parish of Killoughy* (Mullingar 1947); Comerford, M., *Collections Relating to the Dioceses Kildare and Leighlin*, (3 vols, Dublin 1884-6).

## KILLINEY (Co. Dublin)

Negotiations were opened in 1941 for the purchase of a house at Seafield Road from Miss Field. It was intended that the community there would engage in higher studies in Irish history and language, as well as Franciscan history. Dún Mhuire was officially opened in April 1945, although the community were not able to settle in for another year. Extended in 1955 and erected into a guardianate in 1975, Dún Mhuire enjoys considerable standing in the academic world. The de Valera papers are housed there and work is proceeding on cataloguing them.

## KINALEHIN (*alias* Kilnalahan) (Co. Galway)

The site is in the village of Abbey on the Clare-Galway border.
Remains: part of the church, with two chapels; sections of other walls.

This was the only Carthusian priory in Ireland. It was founded by John de Cogan (see under Claregalway) *c.* 1252. The Carthusians did not succeed in establishing their order in Ireland and sold most of 129 their temporalities to the Knights Hospitaller in 1306. In 1321, at the general chapter of the Order, a decision was taken not to send any new monks to the Irish house, thereby allowing it to close in time. By 1341 the Carthusian house was deserted.

In 1371 the archbishop of Tuam noted that the monks would have no objection to friars taking possession of the monastery. By 1400 the Franciscans were busy repairing the building. Protected by the Clanricarde family, the friars remained in residence until the end of the sixteenth century, when they had to move due to the destruction of the building. The Observant reform was introduced in 1611. Except during the Cromwellian period, the community were in residence throughout the seventeenth century, but departed in 1698, because of the Act banishing religious from Ireland. They returned *c.* 1711. There was a community of five in 1766. The last friar was probably John Hughes who lived in Galway just before his death in 1824-5.

Burke, F., *The Abbey of Kilnalahan* (Loughrea 1981).

## LIMERICK (City)

Nothing remains on the mediaeval site at the back of Sir Harry's Mall.

The friary was founded by Thomas de Burgo in 1267, but it is likely that the friars first arrived in Limerick *c.* 1245. The community did not adopt the Observant reform until 1534. The friars went into hiding after the Suppression, but the area around their old building still retained the name 'St Francis Abbey', and the river came to be called the 'Abbey River'.

The friars re-established a formal residence in 1615, with a community of four. On 14 June 1646 the standards which had been captured at the battle of Benburb were displayed in the friary chapel before being deposited in St Mary's Cathedral. The Franciscans were expelled from the city in October 1651, but they soon returned and recovered possession of their chapel in 1687. In 1732 there were four friars in a small residence near the corner of Nicholas Street and Athlunkard Street. By 1766 two friars were also doing parish work in the chapels of St Nicholas and of St Mary. In 1782 the community obtained a site in Newgate Lane, where a small friary and chapel were erected. The Franciscans were forced to leave this site in 1822. They settled in Bank Place for a short time, before acquiring the present (Henry Street) site in 1824. The chapel was completed in 1826 and the friary in 1827. Both buildings were condemned by the visitator general in 1873. Work on new buildings began in 1876. The church was blessed and opened by Bishop Butler on 14 December

1879 and the friary was completed in 1886. However the church was only partially finished and work on an extension began in 1928. It was consecrated by the bishop of Limerick, Dr Keane, on 7 December 1931.

Egan, B., ofm, *Franciscan Limerick* (Limerick 1971).

## LISGOOLE (Co. Fermanagh)

There are no remains on this site on the southern bank of Upper Lough Erne.

The Canons Regular of St Augustine took possession of the site of the early Irish monastery of St Aid *c.* 1145, and built the Abbey of SS Peter, Paul and Mary. This building was burned in 1360 and later rebuilt. Like many other religious houses in Ulster, it escaped suppression. By 1583 the community had dwindled. The abbot, Cahill Mc'Brien Mc'Cuchonnaght Maguire, drew up an agreement, witnessed by many of the Ulster leaders, to hand the abbey over to the Franciscans. It would seem that the friars had not finished reconstructing the building when they were forced to leave in 1598. They returned in 1616 and served in the region through most of the seventeenth and well into the eighteenth centuries. The gradual involvement of the friars in parish work brought about the dispersal of the community. The last Franciscan to live in the area was Fr Stephen Keenan, who died at Enniskillen in 1811. (See also under Monaghan.)

Giblin, C., ofm, 'Lisgoole Friary', *Clogh. Rec.* (1970), 158-66, 183-6.

## LISLAUGHTIN (Co. Kerry)

The site is on the southern side of the Shannon Estuary, near Ballylongford.

Remains: church and transept chapel fairly complete, but tower has fallen; large sections of the convent are also standing; unfortunately the entrance gateway, one of the few which had survived, was knocked recently. Notable feature: a processional cross belonging to the friary is now in the National Museum of Ireland.

The friary was founded for the Observant friars by John O'Connor *c.* 1464. In 1580 it was attacked and three friars killed. The friars fled and did not return to the area until 1629. Later that year, persecution forced some of the friars of Muckross to seek refuge with those who had returned to Lislaughtin. The building was sacked by the Cromwellians in 1652 and the friars went into hiding. They re-emerged *c.* 1660, but seem to have finally abandoned the area early in the eighteenth century.

131

Walsh, K., 'Franciscan Friaries in pre-Reformation Kerry', *JKAHS*, ix (1976), 18-31.

## LOUGH DERG (Co. Donegal)

There was an early Irish monastery on the present Station Island. After *c.* 1130 the Canons Regular of St Augustine took charge of the site but moved the pilgrimage to Saint's Island, where they remained until the Reformation. The Canons had difficulty staffing the sanctuary. In 1631 the archbishop of Armagh officially requested that the Franciscans be given charge of the shrine. It is probable that friars were already working at Lough Derg.

The Franciscans remained in charge during the Cromwellian period and well into the following century. At some time, they changed from Saint's Island back to Station Island. *C.* 1763 they built a small friary and oratory dedicated to Our Lady of the Angels – the title of the famous Franciscan church at Assisi. In 1780 work began on a church dedicated to St Patrick, but the next year falling vocations forced the friars to hand over the shrine to the clergy of the diocese of Clogher.

Giblin, C., ofm, 'The Franciscans in the Diocese of Clogher', *Clogh. Rec.* (1970) 149-203.

## MEELICK (Co. Galway)

The site is about six and a half kilometres from the village of Eyrecourt.

Remains: church and sacristy are still in use; east end of church rebuilt 1860s; traces of transept chapel and friary; a small mill. Notable features: bas-relief of St Francis; many seventeenth century inscriptions.

Papal permission for Meelick friary was granted by the antipope John XXIII in 1414 shortly before he was deposed, probably on the basis of an O'Madden request. Repair work was being carried out in 1445 and again in 1479, when the friary became Observant. Under O'Madden protection, the friary escaped suppression until 1559, when the friars went into hiding, perhaps in the wood of Muckeny, or on Friar's Island. The friars remained in the area and used the friary intermittently during the next one hundred years. During this period it was attacked and pillaged on several occasions.

There were four friars in the community at Meelick during most of the eighteenth century. In addition many friars worked in the parishes of Fahy and Meelick. By the nineteenth century the community had dwindled to two, despite which the church was repaired in 1832. The last friar of Meelick was Fr Bonaventure

Francis Reynolds. After the local landlord took some of the friars' land he withdrew to Athlone in 1848. When he died in November 1852, there was no friar available to replace him.

Mac Fhinn, E., *Mílic* (Dublin 1943).

## MONAGHAN (town)
The exact site is uncertain and there are no surviving remains.

Monaghan was the site of one of the late Conventual foundations, *c.* 1462. It was founded by the MacMahons. Although it had been attacked in 1540, the friary was not evacuated until it was sacked by an English army in 1589, by which time the community had become Observant. The friars returned *c.* 1635 and, apart from the Cromwellian period, continued to reside in the town for most of the seventeenth century. They officially re-opened their friary in 1688. In the first half of the eighteenth century the community gradually dispersed and became involved in parish work.

As the communities associated with the friaries of Monaghan and Lisgoole began to disperse in the mid-eighteenth century, the friars became more involved in parish work. In 1801 fifteen Franciscans were working in the diocese of Clogher in areas such as Ballybay, Donaghmore, Lough Egish and Aughnamullen. The last friars associated with the area were Fr Thomas Martin, who worked around Ballytrain and died in 1849-50, and Fr John McMahon, who lived at Chapel Moyle (Lough Egish) *c.* 1845.

Giblin, C., ofm, 'The Franciscans in the Diocese of Clogher', *Clogh. Rec.* (1970) 149-203.

## MONASTERORIS (Co. Offaly)
The site is in a graveyard about four kilometres west of Edenderry. Remains: most of the church, altered and overgrown with ivy.

The friary was founded in 1325 by John de Bermingham, earl of Louth. Its name is derived from the Irish form of his name (Mac Feorais). The Observant reform was adopted in 1506. Fortified and garrisoned by the O'Moore's the building was severely damaged during a siege by the Lord Lieutenant, the earl of Surrey, in 1521. The friars remained in the area for another fifty years. They returned to the site of their old foundation *c.* 1645. After the expulsion of the friars in Cromwellian times there is little evidence of Franciscan activity until the eighteenth century, when the friars took on parish work in the Rhode-Daingean area. Fr Matthew Walsh, vicar of Daingean, who died in 1794, was the last friar of Monasteroris.

133

Comerford, M., *Collections Relating to the Dioceses of Kildare and Leighlin*, (3 vols, Dublin 1884-6).

## MONS PIETATIS (Co. Mayo)

The site of this Co. Mayo friary has never been satisfactorily identified. It is first mentioned in official documents in 1645, implying a foundation *c*. 1643. Papal approval was sought in 1663 and a superior was appointed in 1672. This is the last real evidence for a Franciscan connection, although the name remained in use during the eighteenth century. Given a strong local tradition, Killedan, west of Kiltimagh, seems the most likely site.

Mooney, C., ofm, 'The Franciscans in Co. Mayo', *JGAHS*, xxviii (1958-9), 52-6, 42-69 .

## MOYNE (Co. Mayo)

The site is on the shore of Killala Bay and should be visited in conjunction with the neighbouring Third Order friary of Rosserk.
Remains: church, chapels, tower and convent are practically complete. Notable feature: reader's desk in refectory window.

Moyne was founded in the late 1450s, possibly at the instigation of Fr Nehemias O'Donohue who, in 1460, became the first vicar provincial of the Irish Observants. Moyne was thus the first Observant foundation in the country. The de Burgos were the major patrons and the church was consecrated in 1462. Building continued for another fifty years. By this time Moyne had become a student house and had a community of about fifty. The friary was raided in 1578-9. The building was destroyed and the community dispersed when it was raided by Sir Richard Bingham in 1590. About six friars remained and they re-opened a formal residence in 1618. After the efforts to expel the religious from Ireland in 1697, the friars seem to have moved to Kilmacshalgan (Co. Sligo), at least for a while, and became involved in parish work. The community of six in 1744 was reduced to two by 1771 and the last friar of Moyne, Fr Thomas Burke, died in 1800. The friars considered returning to the area in 1913.

Mooney, C., ofm, 'The Franciscans in Co. Mayo' in *JGAHS*, xxviii (1958-9), 52-6, 42-69.

## MUCKROSS (*alias* Irrelagh) (Co. Kerry)

The site is a well-known tourist attraction by the Lakes of Killarney.
Remains: the church, transept, chapel, tower and convent are complete.

Donal Mac Carthy Mór founded the friary of Muckross for the

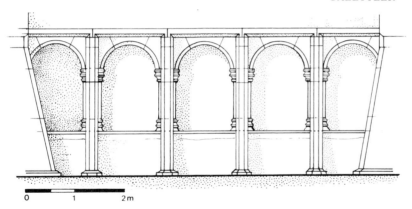

*Cloister arcade, Muckross Friary, Co. Kerry*

Observant friars *c.* 1448. Building continued for nearly fifty years. The friary was dedicated to the Holy Trinity. The community was legally suppressed in 1541, but the friars remained in residence until *c.* 1589, when two friars were killed during an English raid. The Franciscans returned *c.* 1600, and again *c.* 1612. They were once more in residence by 1639, having been driven out on the two previous occasions. The Cromwellians expelled them again in 1652. The friars withdrew to a place of refuge, probably Friar's Glen on the side of Mangerton. *C.* 1760 the few remaining friars moved to a cottage at Faghbawn by the Flesk River. By now the community was reduced to two, yet the friars started a college in 1780 on the site of the present Scott's Hotel in Killarney. This eventually grew into the diocesan college of St Brendan. The last friar, Fr J. FitzGerald, left Killarney *c.* 1849. When the Belgian friars came to Kerry in 1860 Fr FitzGerald was guardian of Waterford friary. He died at Athlone in 1880.

Walsh, K., 'The Franciscan Friaries in pre-Reformation Kerry' in *JKAHS*, ix (1976) 18-31; Moriarty, M. J., *Guide to Muckross Abbey* (Dublin 1948).

## MULTYFARNHAM (Co. Westmeath)

The site is that of the present Franciscan friary.
Remains: the nave, transept chapel and tower are original; the choir and some of the windows are modern.

Founded by the Delamares between 1250 and 1265, the early community received much help from the Nugents. The friars adopted the Observant reform at an early stage. The friary was suppressed in October 1540, but the friars remained under Nugent protection. By 1600 the community numbered eighteen and was one   135

*Franciscan College, Multyfarnham, Co. Westmeath*

of the largest in Ireland. The friary was frequently raided during the Elizabethan wars. On 1 October 1601, Sir Francis Shane destroyed the building and captured eleven of the community. From then until *c.* 1622 the Franciscans of Multyfarnham were subjected to continual harassment. The friars went into hiding during 1651-9 and set up a residence at Knightswood, where there was a community of about ten in 1671. After 1700 the friars became involved in parish work and were able to return to their original building in 1710. The last Franciscan parish prièst of Multyfarnham, Fr Edward Francis Dease, died in 1824. Part of the mediaeval chapel was restored in 1827, and a small residence built on the ruins of the old convent in 1839. On 11 December 1896 the 'Brown' Franciscans took over Multyfarnham as the first reform house in Ireland. Plans were made to open a seraphic college, where candidates for the Order could be educated. St Louis College came into being in 1899. When this college was moved to Gormanston in 1956, Multyfarnham became St Isidore's Agricultural College. It was opened by Mr James Dillon, minister for Agriculture, on 13 November 1956. There have been extensive alterations to the church at Multyfarnham in recent years, both to increase its pastoral effectiveness and to restore its mediaeval flavour. The old choir has been reconstructed as a Eucharistic chapel, opened in 1975. A new agricultural college was opened by Mr Ray McSharry on 28 May 1982.

O'Donnell, T., ofm, *Franciscan Abbey of Multyfarnham* (Multyfarnham 1951); O Gibealláin, P., ofm, *Monuments and Memories* (Multyfarnham 1984).

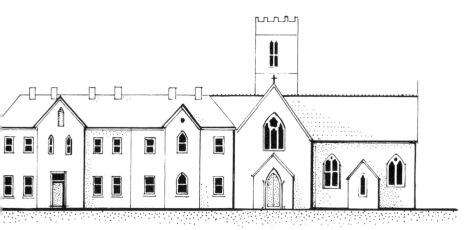

## NENAGH (Co. Tipperary)

The site is on a lane to the south of the main street.

Remains: the church is complete, but the tower has fallen.

Nenagh friary was founded by the O'Kennedys probably before 1252. It later became the principal house of the Gaelic custody within the province. The O'Carrolls burned the town of Nenagh, including the still Conventual friary, in 1548. The friars remained until *c.* 1587, after which no effort was made to set up a residence until 1632, when the Observants came. The friars were expelled by the Cromwellians, but soon returned. A community was still in residence in the early eighteenth century, but had broken up by 1766. Friars continued to work as parish clergy in the area and Fr Patrick Harty died there in 1817 as a quasi-curate. He was the last Franciscan of Nenagh.

Gleeson, D. F. 'The Franciscan Convent at Nenagh' *Molua* (1938), 18-35.

## NEW ROSS (Co. Wexford)

Nothing now remains on the site where the building was pulled down in 1732, although some tomb-slabs from the friary have been re-erected at St Mary's Church.

The earl of Pembroke made a foundation in New Ross for the Crossed friars (Fratres Cruciferi) *c.* 1195. The Franciscan friars came to the town *c.* 1250. When a drunken Crossed friar killed a townsman, the citizens drove his Order from the town and gave their building to the Franciscans. The community remained Conventual until 1558, when the friars were finally expelled. The Observants established a residence in 1615. They were expelled during the Cromwellian period, but soon returned and remained for another century. The friars got a cottage in the town *c.* 1725 and added a chapel in 1729. There were four in residence in 1731, and three in 1744. But the last left within the next decade.

Cullen, J. B., 'The Convent of Ross' *IER* xvii (1921) 42-53; Grannell, F., ofm, *The Franciscans in Wexford*, (Wexford n.d.).

**A** *Nave*
**B** *Choir*
**E** *Sacristy*
**F** *Transept*
**G** *Cloister Garth*
**H** *Tower*
**I** *West Doorway*
**K** *Kitchen*
**L** *Dormitory*
**N** *Refectory*
**O** *Necessarium*
**P** *Day Room*

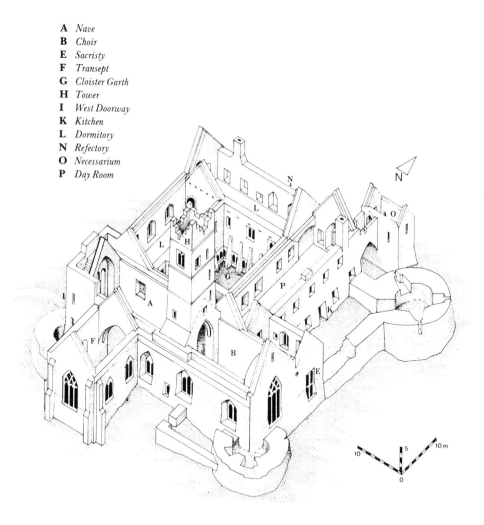

*Quin Friary, Co. Clare: an isometric view.*
*The fifteenth-century friary was built on the ruins of a twelfth-century castle.*

## QUIN (Co. Clare)

The site is on the edge of the village, behind the Catholic church.

Remains: church, tower, transept chapel, convent and some outbuildings are complete; the cloister is one of the best preserved in the country; the ruins of the old castle which pre-dated it have been skilfully incorporated into the friary. Notable features: many fifteenth to nineteenth century tombstones; the large tomb of the Butlers of Dunboyne is in the room beside the refectory. To the east of the friary are the remains of a deserted mediaeval village.

Quin was founded for the Observants by Sioda Cam MacNamara in 1433. It was built on the ruins of a de Clare castle founded in 1280. Under O'Brien protection the friars remained in occupation after the suppression. Despite the partial destruction of the building in 1583, the friars did not depart, but repaired the damage. There was a small community of three living there in 1615. Three friars were killed in an attack on the building in 1651, after which the remaining friars withdrew for some years. On their return the friars worked in Quin until the mid-eighteenth century when they moved to a house at nearby Drim. There were three friars at Drim in 1766, working as parish clergy. The last friar of Quin, Fr John Hogan, worked at Drim until his death in 1820.

Walsh, P. M., ofm, *The Old Friaries of Ennis and Quin* (Wexford 1959).

## ROSCOMMON (town)

The friars were invited to Roscommon in 1269, but had to leave the following year when their house was destroyed by fire and their benefactor had died.

## ROSCREA (Co. Tipperary)

The remains now form the gateway to the grounds of the Catholic church.

Remains: the tower still stands, as do large sections of the church.

Roscrea was a late Conventual foundation, established before 1477. The surviving building dates to 1490-8, when the friary was re-built by Molrony O'Carroll and his wife, Bibiana. The community escaped suppression until 1579, when two friars were captured during an English raid. One was killed, the other abandoned his religion. He was re-converted by Fr Donagh Mooney during a mission and remained a friar until his death. An Observant residence was set up in Roscrea c. 1645 and lasted for about a hundred years, though abandoned during the Cromwellian period, 1650-8, and again from 1670-89.

Gwynn, A., and Gleeson, D. F., *A History of the Diocese of Killaloe* Vol. I, (Dublin 1962).

## ROSS (Rosseriall Friary, Co. Galway)

The site is in a bog half a kilometre west of the village of Headford. Remains: the church, tower, chapels and convent are almost complete; there is evidence of large-scale alterations in the eighteenth century.

Little is known of the early history of Ross friary, though it is probable that it was founded in 1498 for the Observants. Protected by the Clanricarde family, the friars were able to remain after the suppression despite several plunderings and the occupation of the friary by English forces in 1596. In 1616 there was a community of six priests and two brothers in the old building. In 1641 the guardian saved the survivors of an English party of travellers who had been attacked by the Irish near Shrule. The friars were forced to go into hiding during the Cromwellian period. The friary was sacked in 1656. The friars had returned by 1661 and did not leave again until the attempted general expulsion of religious in 1697. They were again in residence by 1711 when their protector was Lord St George. At some stage they had withdrawn to Friar's Island, but through the generosity of a Mr Lynch, the friars were able to build a new house at the foot of Kilroe Hill. There was a community of seven living at Kilroe in 1766, but this had fallen to three by 1801. There were still three friars in the community when the friary was closed by order of the provincial in 1832.

Burke, O. J., *The Abbey of Ross* (Dublin 1868); Mooney, C., ofm, 'The Friary of Ross', *JGAHS*, xxix (1960-1), 7-14.

## ROSSNOWLAGH (Co. Donegal)

During the celebrations to mark the tercentenary of the death of Br Micheál Ó Cléirigh it was suggested that the Franciscans should return to Donegal. Encouraged by the bishop, Dr MacNeely, the friars took up the suggestion. A site was chosen in 1946 near Br Micheál's native area of Kilbarron. The first community lived in Nissen huts until the new friary and church were built. These were officially blessed and dedicated on 29 June 1952. The friary became a full guardianate in 1954 and has since established a Franciscan presence over a wide area. The priests are extremely busy during the summer when crowds flock across the border for confessions and blessings.

O'Byrne, S., ofm, *Franciscan Rossnowlagh* (2nd ed., Rossnowlagh 1978).

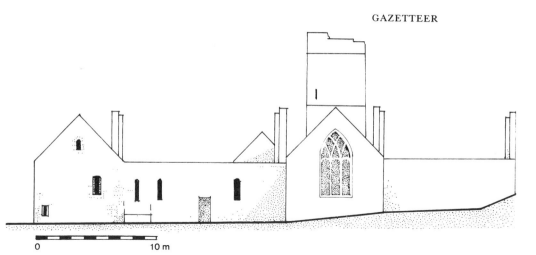

*West elevation, Sherkin Island Friary, Co. Cork*

## SHERKIN ISLAND (Co. Cork)

There is a regular boat service to the island from Baltimore.
Remains: church, tower and transept still stand, as does most of the convent; however some inner walls have been knocked down.

Permission to found an Observant friary was given by Rome to Finighin O'Driscoll in 1449. However, it was after 1462 when friars actually arrived. The friary became the burial place of the O'Driscolls. In 1537 the citizens of Waterford burned the building in retaliation for acts of piracy by the O'Driscolls. The great bell of the friary was on display in Waterford as late as 1615. The friars remained in residence until the island was garrisoned by the English following the battle of Kinsale, but they soon returned and, except during the period of Cromwellian persecution, were active throughout the seventeenth and well into the eighteenth centuries. The last friar, Fr Patrick Hayes, died soon after 1766.

Collins, J. T., 'An Island Friary', J. O'Callaghan (ed.), *Franciscan Cork* (Cork 1953).

## SLANE (Co. Meath)

The site was the little church and hermitage of St Erc.

In addition to a Third Order friary and a college with Capuchin associations on the Hill of Slane itself, there is evidence of a small Franciscan First Order community in the hermitage during 1648-50.

## STRABANE (Co. Tyrone)

There is some evidence for a friary a few kilometres east of the town from the time of the Restoration (1660s) to early in the eighteenth  141 century. The foundations cannot have been very large or significant.

## STRADBALLY (Co. Laois)

There are no significant remains on the site at the back of the convent school.

The early history of the friars in Stradbally is confusing. The building was erected by Lord O'Moore *c*. 1447 for the Conventual friars. The friary escaped suppression until 1569, probably due to its small size. After its suppression the community went into hiding. Three of them were discovered in 1588 and were hanged, drawn and quartered near Abbeyleix. Two friars returned to the area in 1642, but were forced to leave during the Cromwellian persecution. There seems to have been no serious effort to return to the area after this.

Comerford, M., *Collections Relating to the Dioceses of Kildare and Leighlin* (3 vols, Dublin 1884-6).

## STRADE (Co. Mayo)

Jordan de Exeter, lord of Athelthane, founded a friary for the Franciscans at Strade in the mid-thirteenth century. In 1252 his son Stephen gave the site to the Dominicans at the instigation of his wife Basilia, daughter of Miler de Bermingham who was a major patron of the Dominican Order.

Mooney, C., 'The Franciscans in County Mayo', *JGAHS*, xxviii (1958-9), 42-69.

## THURLES (town)

The site was initially beside the cathedral; later in Friar Street, where parts of the oratory still stand.

In 1714 the friars of Cashel were renting a house in Thurles from the Matthews family. By 1740 the community seems to have moved permanently from Cashel to Thurles. There were usually two or three friars living in a small cottage with a private oratory. There was no public church. The friars helped out at the cathedral. In 1787-8 they gave their original site to the Ursulines and moved to Friar Street. The most famous friar in Thurles during the nineteenth century was Fr James (Theodosius) McNamara, who lived there from 1834 to his death in 1881. Efforts to close the residence in Thurles in 1859 were strongly resisted by the archbishop. By then the friars had become chaplains to the workhouse. A decision to close the house was taken at the provincial chapter in 1892 and the last friar of Thurles, Fr Pacificus Doggette, was moved to Multyfarnham.

Conlan, P., ofm, 'The Franciscan House in Thurles', *NMAJ*, xix (1977), 43-9.

## TIMOLEAGUE (Co. Cork)

The site is on a headland in Courtmacsherry Bay on the eastern side of the village of Timoleague.

Remains: church, tower, transept and aisle are complete; large sections of the convent still stand, including parts of the cloister arcade.

There is conflicting evidence about the foundation of this friary. It was founded before 1316 by either Donal Glas Mac Carthy, lord of Carberry, or by William de Barry. It is possible that both were co-founders. The site is on or near the early Irish monastery of Tigh-mo-Laga, from which it takes its name. It became the burial place of the McCarthy's Reagh. It was one of the earliest houses to adopt the Observant reform, in 1460. The building underwent considerable expansion and alteration over the centuries, for example the tower was added c. 1510. The friars remained in residence, under McCarthy protection, after the suppression, though they were occasionally driven out by raids during the Elizabethan wars. The friary was extensively repaired in 1604. In 1629 Br Micheál Ó Cléirigh stayed there copying mss (including the *Book of Lismore*). The friars were again forced to flee during the Cromwellian period and took refuge at nearby Cloggagh. After the Restoration they returned once again. The community was dispersed by the mid-eighteenth century, but individual friars continued to work in the area. The last of these was Fr Bonaventure Tobin, who died c. 1822. Timoleague friary is popularly associated with the Irish poem by Seán Ó Coileáin, *Oidhche dham go doiligh, dubhach* . . . , which is a translation of an English poem by Fr Mathew Horgan.

Collins, J. T., 'The Friary at Timoleague' in J. O'Callaghan ofm (ed.), *Franciscan Cork* (Cork 1953); Coombes, J., *Timoleague and Barrymore* (Timoleague 1969).

## TRIM (Co. Meath)

There are no remains at this site which was near the bridge over the river Boyne.

The first known reference to the Franciscan friary at Trim dates from 1318. However, the friary was founded in the late thirteenth century and was probably in existence by 1282. In 1330, and again c. 1430, the buildings were badly damaged by Boyne floods. The community adopted the Observant reform before 1506. The friars were expelled from Trim in 1542 and did not return until 1629. By the eighteenth century they had become involved in parish work on a large scale (see under Courtown).

Callery, P., 'The Grey Friary of Trim', *IER*, ii (1913), 473-90.

## WATERFORD (City)

The mediaeval site known as 'The French Church' is about half a kilometre from the present friary.

Remains: the church, tower and parts of the transept chapel are complete. Notable feature: the collection of mediaeval statues from the friary previously kept in the Holy Ghost Hospital and now in private hands.

Waterford Friary was one of the first in Ireland, being founded by Sir Hugh Purcell *c.* 1240. It was the scene of the surrender of four Irish chieftains (the O'Connor Don, de Burgo, O'Brien and O'Kennedy) to Richard II in 1395. The community did not adopt the Observant reform until 1521. The friary was suppressed on 2 April 1540, but the friars remained in the city. Henry VIII granted a charter in 1544 to convert part of the building into a hospital-cum-alms-house, this being the original Holy Ghost Hospital. In 1695 the Corporation granted the building to Huguenot refugees, who used it as a church and burial ground. Since then it has been popularly known as 'The French Church'. It was later used by Waterford Methodists who built a church on the site of the convent.

Following suppression, the friars went into hiding in Johnstown, although some of them acted as chaplains to the Holy Ghost Hospital. An official residence was set up in 1612. The friars were forced out of the town in 1652, but returned to Johnstown in 1660. The community was reduced to two or three friars who helped in the parish church, as they had no friary church. In addition individual friars became parish clergy in other parts of the diocese. The residence was changed to the area of South Parade and Water Street *c.* 1790. The friars moved to their present site in 1830 and opened a small chapel and residence in 1835. The church was expanded in 1905-8 and again in 1931-3. It was consecrated in 1944. The present friary was built in 1928. In 1977 one of the friars took up a post as chaplain to the Industrial Estate in Waterford. The following year the friars took over the pastoral charge of Ardkeen General Hospital. Recently a friar has become involved in housing projects and some have lived in a house to give witness to poverty.

Mooney, C., ofm, 'The Franciscans in Waterford' in *JCHAS* , lxix (1964) 73-93; McLeod, C., 'Medieval Figure Sculpture in Ireland: Statues in the Holy Ghost Hospital, Waterford', *JRSAI*, lxxvi (1946) 89-100.

## WEXFORD (town)

Nothing remains of the mediaeval building; the present friary occupies the site.

Little is known of the early history of Wexford friary. It was founded c. 1265 and the community adopted the Observant reform in 1486. After the friary was suppressed in 1540 the friars went into hiding. A small residence was set up in High Street in 1615 and a thatched chapel was opened in 1620. Seven members of the community were killed when the Cromwellians captured Wexford in 1649. Another four friars were killed in 1655. The community was able to return in 1660 and the chapel was re-opened in 1673. A new church was built on the old mediaeval site in 1690 and it was the only Catholic church open in Wexford in the Penal era.

During the eighteenth century the friars were no longer involved in parish work. They ran an academy or secondary school for a while early in the nineteenth century. This was replaced by the present St Peter's College. Down the years the seventeenth century church underwent frequent alterations, especially c. 1790 and in 1857. The present friary was built in 1803 and served both as the residence of the provincial and as the novitiate for much of the first half of the nineteenth century. The 'Brown' friars introduced the reform into Wexford in 1918. The friars were incorporated in the general pastoral scheme which became operative in Wexford in the 1980s. Due to extensive rot, major reconstruction of the church had to be undertaken and it was re-opened on 4 October 1987.

Giblin, A., ofm, *The History and Traditions of Wexford Friary* (Wexford 1969); Grannell, F., ofm, *The Franciscans in Wexford* (Wexford n.d.).

## WICKLOW (town)

The site is in the garden of the parish priest's residence.
Remains: parts of the church and transept.

The friary of Wicklow was founded c. 1265. According to local tradition it was built in thanksgiving for a victory over the FitzGeralds by the O'Tooles and O'Byrnes. It is not certain when the community adopted the Observant reform, nor when the friars had to leave the district. By 1615, we know that the area had been long deserted by the friars. They returned c. 1635, were expelled by the Cromwellians, and returned again in 1659. However, Franciscan life in Wicklow died out early in the eighteenth century.

Millett, B., ofm, 'The Franciscans in County Wicklow', *Arch. Fran. Hist.*, lxxvii (1984).

## YOUGHAL (Co. Cork)

The site is now occupied by the Presentation Convent. There are no significant remains.

According to tradition the first friars to arrive in Ireland landed at Youghal and made their first foundation in the town. Work on a permanent building began under the patronage of Maurice FitzGerald, justiciar of Ireland, *c.* 1235. In 1290 the friary was the scene of an unusual incident when the sheriff raided it to seize goods which had been left in the safe-keeping of the friars. This was done to pay the taxes of the owner of the goods, John le Juvene. In 1460 Youghal became one of the first houses to adopt the Observant reform. Despite being officially suppressed in 1541, the friars remained in or near their old building until 1583, when it was destroyed by the English. The community probably withdrew to a place of refuge at Curraheen, but were able to re-establish a residence in Youghal in 1627. Forced out by the Cromwellians, the friars soon returned. However, the difficulties of living in Youghal during the Penal period forced them to move to Co. Waterford (see under Curraheen).

O'Sullivan, D., 'Youghal, the first house of the Friars Minor in Ireland' in J. O'Callaghan (ed.), *Franciscan Cork* (Cork 1953).

*Owl, Kilconnell Friary, Co. Galway*

# II
# IRISH FRANCISCAN SITES
# IN EUROPE

## BALLABEG (Bymacan, Isle of Man)

The site is on a farm outside the village.
Remains: most of the church and parts of the convent.

William Montague, earl of Salisbury, founded a friary for Irish Franciscans on a neglected part of his estate. As there was no other Franciscan foundation in the diocese of Sodor, Pope Urban V granted the Irish friars permission for a foundation at Ballabeg on 7 December 1367. The church was consecrated in 1373. The initial community numbered twelve friars. In later years two Irish friars became bishops of Man. The community seem to have dispersed and ceased to function following the suppression of the friary in 1540.

Barratt, J. K., 'The Franciscan Friary of Bymacan', *Jn. Manx Museum*, vi (1964), 203-13.

## BOULAY (Lorraine, France)

The site is to the north of the main square of the town.
Remains: parts of some walls and large sections of the gardens.

A château at Boulay, which belonged to the duke of Lorraine, was ruined by fire in 1695. The Act expelling religious from Ireland was then about to become law. Two Irish friars, Frs Bernardine Gavan and Bernardine Plunket, independently discovered that the duke was sympathetic to an Irish foundation. Strict conditions imposed by the bishop of Metz had discouraged German friars, but Fr Plunket applied for permission to make a foundation in 1698. The legalities took two years to complete and it was not until 1700 that the Irish Franciscans could take over the ruined building. The initial community of six increased to about twenty-five and the château was gradually converted into a college. The great hall became the refectory. In addition to its role as an Irish student house, the college at Boulay became a centre for local pastoral action and the friars ran a school for local youth. Two-thirds of the community had to speak German. In 1790, during the French Revolution, soldiers were billeted in the college. It was then turned into a place of retirement for elderly religious, and was finally closed for Catholic use in October 1792. After the Revolution efforts were made to recover the college, but lack of finance proved a major difficulty. Money to compensate the friars got lost in a bureaucratic wrangle between the British and French governments.

Mooney, C., ofm, *Irish Franciscans and France* (Dublin 1964).

## CAPRANICA (Province of Viterbo, Italy)

The old buildings are still being used by the Irish Franciscans.

The church here was built in 1551 by the Society of Hunters to house the picture of Our Lady painted by Andrea Vanni *c.* 1340.

The Hermits of St Augustine took over the church in 1559 and added the convent. They let the building go to ruin and it partially collapsed in 1632, as a result of which they abandoned it in 1652.

Fr Luke Wadding, the founder of St Isidore's College in Rome, had been looking for a small house outside Rome for the Irish Franciscans. Having first considered San Antonio in Casale, he applied for Capranica and obtained it as a holiday house and novitiate in 1656. The extensive repairs which were necesary took until 1663 to complete. By then the community numbered fifteen. During the eighteenth century there was a small community at Capranica which still served as a notivitiate, in addition to St Isidore's. It was taken over by the French forces who occupied Rome in 1798 and was not recovered until 1814. It was then rented to a local landlord, who provided a priest to say mass on the major feasts. The revenue from Capranica served to keep St Isidore's open. In 1853 Capranica returned to its original function as a novitiate, but did not become of major importance until the period of the Doebbing reform. In 1890 Fr Doebbing was appointed delegate general for Capranica and began using it as a house of formation. It also served as a seraphic college training candidates for the Irish province. Irish and German friars began an active apostolate in the area. Capranica was returned to full Irish control and, in 1906, the Irish definitorium made a formal decision to retain it as part of the Irish province. Since then it has functioned as a holiday house for St Isidore's, with Italian Franciscans staffing the church, and in charge since 1921. A small house was completed in 1986 as a residence for the friars in place of the old building.

Conlan, P., ofm, *St Isidore's, Rome* (Rome 1982), 103-25

## CASTEL SANT' ELIA (Province of Viterbo, Italy)

This former hermitage was taken over by the Irish friars in 1892. Fr Doebbing acted as delegate general. Together with Rome and Capranica, it was used to house friars engaged in the reform of the Irish province. The Irish withdrew in 1898 and Sant'Elia became the responsibility of the German province of Saxony. They have since enlarged the convent and made it a major place of pilgrimage in honour of Our Lady. It was transferred to Polish religious by the German friars in 1981.

Conlan, P., ofm, *St Isidore's, Rome* (Rome 1982), 201-3

## LOUVAIN (now Leuven, Belgium)

The College of St Anthony is now the Irish Institute for European Affairs.

The Irish minister provincial, Fr Florence Conry, used his influence with Philip III of Spain to establish an Irish Franciscan College in the Low Countries. Permission was given in 1606 and papal approval was granted in 1607. The friars tried a number of locations in Louvain before settling on the present site, where the foundation stone of St Anthony's College was laid on 9 May 1617. Louvain, the first of the Irish Franciscan continental colleges, became a major centre for Irish studies in the seventeenth century. Although the friars of the Louvain school are best known for their works on Irish history, they also produced many religious works in Irish. The activities of the college were slightly curtailed by the anti-religious decrees of Emperor Joseph II in 1782. During the French Revolution the college was temporarily closed by the revolutionary government in 1793. Over the next few years the guardian, Fr James Cowan, struggled to keep the building in Irish hands. It was finally sold in 1822. Much valuable manuscript material had already been confiscated and is still held in Brussels. The remainder was sent either to Rome or to Wexford.

After a century of use as a school for underprivileged children, the college came on the market again in 1922 and was purchased for the Irish friars in 1925. The first community moved in during 1926, but extensive renovations delayed a formal opening until 30 June 1927. Due to the German invasion of Belgium the college was evacuated in May 1940 and during the war years Belgian friars were in charge of it. It was returned to Irish control in 1948 and once again became a residence for undergraduate and postgraduate students. After 1969 friars of the community in Louvain provided facilities for English-speaking Catholics in Brussels, including Sunday mass. This arrangement was formalized into a regular chaplaincy in 1972 and the Irish Franciscans have pastoral charge of the English and Irish Catholic population in Brussels.

In 1967 the original university was split into two, a Flemish campus in Leuven and a French one twenty kilometres to the south. This, combined with a fall in vocations greatly limited the role of St Anthony's. During the next decade the community dwindled and the

149

house ceased to be a guardianate in 1981. It was decided to use the buildings as an Irish Institute for European Affairs. A project director was appointed in April 1983 and the Institute was formally inaugurated in December 1983. Reconstruction work began on the building in June 1984 and shortly afterwards a small new friary was built to maintain a Franciscan presence. The friars also renovated the church. The first courses began in March 1985 and the Institute is now well established.

Conlan, P., ofm, *St Anthony's College of the Irish Franciscans at Louvain*, (Dublin 1977); Mooney, C., ofm, 'St Anthony's College, Louvain', *Don. Ann.*, viii (1969), 14-48; Jordan, K., ofm, 'St Anthony's in Louvain', *Fran. Coll. Ann.* (Multyfarnham 1987).

## PARIS (France)

The Irish Franciscans sought many times to obtain a residence in Paris for friars who wished to study at the University. These efforts were opposed by the French friars, who ran an international hostel. There was an Irish Franciscan house in Paris for a short period after 1617, from 1621 to 1627 and again from 1653 to 1668. In 1810 an attempt by the French government to set up an English-speaking seminary, which would include the Irish friars, failed.

Mooney, C., ofm, *Irish Franciscans and France* (Dublin 1964).

## PRAGUE (Czechoslovakia)

Most of the house and the church are still standing on Hybernska.

In 1628 Fr Malachy Fallon was sent to Vienna from the overcrowded college at Louvain to obtain another Irish Franciscan foundation from the emperor. He found a suitable site in Prague and in 1630 a group set out for the city to found what became the largest of the Irish Franciscan continental colleges, the College of the Immaculate Conception at Prague. The building was formally opened on 6 July 1631. During the next century it continued to expand. The foundation-stone of a new church was laid in 1652, while extra wings were added in 1704 and in 1739. The college was suppressed by direct order of Emperor Joseph II on 29 August 1786, at which time there were thirty-seven friars in residence. Six old friars were allowed to stay on in Prague, with government pensions, until they died. The buildings became government property and are now used as an exhibition centre.

Millett, B., ofm, *The Irish Franciscans 1651-65* (Rome 1964); Jennings, B., ofm, 'The Irish Franciscans in Prague', *Studies* (1939), 210-22.

## ROME (Italy)

The College of St Isidore is still used by the Irish Franciscans.

Fr Luke Wadding arrived in Rome as an official Spanish emissary in 1617 and began to look for an Irish Franciscan house in the Eternal City. A group of Spanish Discalced Franciscans had begun the erection of a friary dedicated to St Isidore the Farmer of Madrid in the year of his canonization, 1622. Due to financial problems, the Spanish friars withdrew and went to live at Ara Coeli, the residence of the minister general. Fr Wadding petitioned for the use of the building and it was granted to the Irish friars by decree of the minister general on 13 June 1625. Pope Urban VIII issued the Bull of Foundation on 20 October. From then until his death in 1657, Fr Wadding laboured to expand the college. He also founded the Irish Pastoral College. Major restoration work was done at St Isidore's *c.* 1750. The building was seized by the invading French in 1798-9 and again in 1810. On this occasion the college was turned into tenements and many of the rooms were let to a group of artists known as the 'Nazarenes'. The guardian, Fr James McCormick, remained in residence and regained control of the college in October 1814. Restoration work was again carried out in 1856 and *c.* 1890. Following the appointment of Fr Bernard Doebbing as lecturer and master at St Isidore's, the college became a centre for the reform of the Irish friars in the late nineteenth century. It later reverted to Irish control. Students were normally trained in theology by lecturers living in the college. Since the Second World War they have begun to attend outside universities in Rome. Although cut off from Ireland during the Second World War, the college was able to remain active and is still the main house of theological training for the Irish Franciscans.

Conlan, P., ofm, *St Isidore's, Rome* (Rome 1982); Daly, A., ofm, *S. Isidoro* (Rome 1971).

## WIELUN (south-east Poland)

Exact site and present condition unknown; parts believed to exist.

In the mid-seventeenth century the Irish friars had sought to make a foundation at Danzig or Poznan, but were prevented from doing so by the king of Poland. Friars of the province of St Anthony took pity on the Irish and offered them the friary of the Annunciation at Wielun on 16 July 1645. The arrangement was approved by the minister general in 1646 and the first community seems to have come from Louvain. The Polish friars requested the return of their friary in 1653 and the Irish friars complied with the request.

Millett, B., ofm, *The Irish Franciscans 1651-65* (Rome 1964); Jennings, B., ofm, 'The Irish Franciscans in Poland', *Arch. Hib.*, xx (1957), 38-56.

# Appendix
# Irish Franciscan Ministers Provincial

This list gives the actual rulers of the Irish Franciscan province whether they were a provincial elected by chapter or appointed by the minister general, a vicar provincial appointed after the death of a provincial, or an Observant vicar provincial. From *c.* 1460 to 1518 a Conventual minister provincial ruled the province with a vicar provincial to look after the Observants. From 1518 there were two Irish provinces until the Conventuals disappeared at the Reformation.

| | |
|---|---|
| Richard of Ingworth | 1230-1239 |
| John Keating | 1239-1254 |
| Deodatus – | 1254- |
| Gilbert of Slane (or Clane) | 1266- |
| John Tancard | 1270-1272 |
| Thomas of Swinesfield | 1272-1279 |
| John – | 1279-1282 |
| Matthew – | -1282- |
| William of Tadyngton | 1294- |
| Thomas Thorpe | -1301-05- |
| Thomas Godman | -1316- |
| Henry (Cogery?) | 1322- |
| John Fitzralph | -1332 |
| Stephen Barry | -1336- |
| Gerald Lagles (Lawless?) | -1353 |
| John Tonebrigg | 1353- |
| Hugh Bernard | -1358-59- |
| Tadhg Brazil | -1369 |
| Michael | -1382 |
| John (Wabergen?) | -1405- |
| John While (or White) | -1441 |
| John Knoker | 1441- |
| Edmond Fitzgerald | -1444- |
| William O'Reilly | 1445-1448 |
| David Carew | 1448-1448 |
| Nicholas Walsh | 1448-1448 |
| Gilbert Walsh | 1448- |
| William O'Reilly | -1450-54- |

## Conventual Ministers Provincial

| | |
|---|---|
| William O'Reilly | -1465-69- |

| | |
|---|---|
| Thaddeus O'Donohue | 1471- |
| Maurice O'Fihely | -1506 |
| Richard Clynton | -1538- |
| Anthony Alarcon | 1556- |
| Jerome Fiorati of Ferrara (titular) | 1564- |

## Observant Vicars Provincial

| | |
|---|---|
| Malachy O'Clune | -1460 |
| Nehemias O'Donohue | 1460-1462 |
| Dermot O'Cannon | 1462-1463 |
| Donagh O'Cullenan | 1463-1466 |
| Malachy O'Clune | 1466-1468 |
| Dermot Fogarty | 1468-1469 |
| Donal Thomas | 1469-1472 |
| Donal O'Fallon | 1472-1475 |
| Donal Thomas | 1475-1478 |
| Tadhg O'Malley | 1478-1484 |
| Nicholas Mac Narry | 1484-1489 |
| Donal Thomas | 1489-1492 |
| John Jarnigon | 1492-1494 |
| Philip O'Maighreain | 1494-1497 |
| Patrick O'Hely | 1497-1500 |
| Philip O'Maighreain | 1500-1504 |
| Conor Mac Hugh | 1504-1507 |
| William O'Niallain | 1507-1510 |
| Flann O'Daly | 1510-1513 |
| Philip O'Maighreain | 1513-1518 |

## Franciscan (Observant) Ministers Provincial

| | |
|---|---|
| William O'Maighreain | 1518-1521 |
| David O'Herlihy | 1521-1524 |
| Clement O'Caollaidhe | 1524-1527 |
| Timothy Thomas | 1527-1530 |
| David O'Herlihy | 1530-1533 |
| Bernard Conry | 1533-1534 |
| Timothy Thomas | 1534-1537 |
| Terence O'Connor | 1537-1540 |
| Patrick O'Maolain | 1540-1543 |
| Dermot (Mac Eoin?) | 1543-1544 |
| Terence O'Connor | 1544-1548 |
| Patrick O'Hogan | 1548-1552 |
| Farrell MacEgan | 1553-1555 |
| Patrick O'Maolain | 1555-1556 |
| John Corcoran | 1557-1561 |

| | |
|---|---|
| Farrell MacEgan | 1561-1564 |
| Patrick O'Hogan | 1564-1567 |
| Walter MacQuaid | 1567-1570 |
| John Gallagher | 1570-1573 |
| Richard Brady | 1573-1576 |
| John O'Gowan | 1577-1580 |
| Eoghan O'Duffy | 1580-1583 |
| Brian O'Féighery | 1583-1587 |
| Walter MacQuaid | 1587-1590 |
| Cormac O'Gowan | 1590-1593 |
| Patrick Kennan | 1593-1596 |
| Columban Lennon | 1596-1599 |
| John Grey | 1599-1602 |
| Edmond O'Mullarkey | 1602-1606 |
| Florence Conry | 1606-1609 |
| Maurice Dunleavy | 1609-1612 |
| Francis Colman O'Mellaghlin | 1612-1615 |
| Donagh Mooney | 1615-1618 |
| Eoghan Field | 1618-1621 |
| Nicholas Shea | 1621-1625 |
| Francis O'Mahony (Matthews?) | 1625-1629 |
| Valentine Browne | 1629-1632 |
| Henry O'Mellan | 1632-1635 |
| Joseph Everard | 1635-1638 |
| John Barnewall | 1638-1641 |
| Anthony McGeoghegan | 1641-1644 |
| Brian Conny (Mac Giolla Coinne) | 1644-1647 |
| Thomas McKiernan | 1647-1650 |
| Francis O'Sullivan | 1650-1653 |
| Bernardine Barry | 1653-1654 |
| Bonaventure Mellaghlin | 1654-1655 |
| Francis O'Farrell | 1655-1658 |
| Brian MacEgan | 1658-1661 |
| Anthony Doherty | 1661-1666 |
| Francis Coppinger | 1666-1669 |
| Peter Gaynor | 1669-1672 |
| Bernard Kelly | 1672-1675 |
| John Brady | 1675-1678 |
| Eoghan Callanan | 1678-1682 |
| James Darcy | 1682-1684 |
| Anthony Burke | 1684-1687 |
| Francis O'Neill | 1687-1690 |
| Edmond Dullany | 1690-1694 |
| John Baptist O'Donnell | 1694-1697 |

| | |
|---|---|
| Anthony Kelly | 1697-1700 |
| Bonaventure Collyn (MacCollin?) | 1700-1703 |
| Bonaventure Oliver Fitzgerald | 1703-1706 |
| Peter Warren | 1706-1709 |
| John Burke | 1709-1714 |
| Anthony O'Donnell | 1714-1717 |
| Anthony MacNamara | 1717-1720 |
| Francis Delamere | 1720-1724 |
| Anthony MacHugo | 1724-1727 |
| Francis Stuart | 1727-1730 |
| Lawrence Ryan | 1730-1733 |
| Bonaventure Mandeville | 1733-1736 |
| Patrick Brown | 1736-1739 |
| Francis Maguire | 1739-1742 |
| Lewis O'Donnell | 1742-1745 |
| Bonaventure Paye | 1745-1748 |
| Francis French | 1748-1751 |
| Bernardine O'Reilly | 1751-1754 |
| Francis Deady | 1754-1757 |
| Christopher Barnewall | 1757-1760 |
| Christopher French | 1760-1763 |
| James MacDonnell | 1763-1766 |
| John Bonaventure O'Brien | 1766-1769 |
| Christopher Fleming | 1769-1772 |
| Anthony French | 1772-1776 |
| Dominick MacDavett | 1776-1779 |
| James Lewis O'Donnell | 1779-1782 |
| Bernard Brady | 1782-1785 |
| John Anthony Kennedy | 1785-1788 |
| James O'Reilly | 1788-1791 |
| Lawrence Callanan | 1791-1794 |
| Bernard Brady | 1794-1801 |
| Anthony Coen | 1801-1803 |
| Patrick Lambert | 1803-1804 |
| Bonaventure Stewart | 1804-1807 |
| Michael Collins | 1807-1811 |
| James Flinn | 1811-1815 |
| Anthony Garrahan | 1815-1819 |
| James Cowan | 1819-1822 |
| William Aloysius O'Meara | 1822-1825 |
| John Francis Dunne | 1825-1827 |
| Joseph Murphy | 1827-1828 |
| Philip Anthony Lyons | 1828-1831 |
| Anthony Nugent Dardis | 1831-1834 |

| | |
|---|---|
| Edmund Paschal Hogan | 1834-1837 |
| Henry Hughes | 1837-1840 |
| Bonaventure McDonnell | 1840-1842 |
| Joseph Killian | 1842-1843 |
| James Walsh | 1843-1844 |
| Edmund Paschal Hogan | 1844-1846 |
| Patrick Anthony McCabe | 1846-1849 |
| Clement Anthony Reville | 1849-1852 |
| Anthony Nugent Dardis | 1852-1854 |
| Edmund Paschal Hogan | 1854-1858 |
| Gregory Lawrence Cosgrove | 1858-1864 |
| Michael Aloysius Cavanagh | 1864-1867 |
| Philip Dominic Kehoe | 1867-1873 |
| Gregory Lawrence Cosgrove | 1873-1876 |
| Clement Anthony Reville | 1876-1877 |
| Philip Dominic Kehoe | 1877-1879 |
| Richard Augustine Hill | 1879-1882 |
| John Alphonsus-Marie Jackman | 1882-1888 |
| Patrick Joseph Cleary | 1888-1895 |
| John Alphonsus-Marie Jackman | 1895-1899 |
| Peter Begley | 1899-1902 |
| Lewis Baldwin | 1902-1903 |
| Benignus Gannon | 1903-1905 |
| Leo Sheehan | 1905-1908 |
| Benignus Gannon | 1908-1911 |
| John Capistran Hanrahan | 1911-1912 |
| Nicholas Dillon | 1912-1918 |
| John Capistran Hanrahan | 1918-1920 |
| Dominic Enright | 1920-1924 |
| Hubert Quinn | 1924-1930 |
| Flannan O'Neill | 1930-1936 |
| Augustine O'Neill | 1936-1942 |
| John Evangelist McBride | 1942-1949 |
| Pacificus Nolan | 1949-1951 |
| Hubert Quinn | 1951-1959 |
| Jarlath Mangan | 1959-1960 |
| Celsus O'Brien | 1960-1972 |
| Louis Brennan | 1972-1979 |
| David O'Reilly | 1979-1987 |
| Fiachra Ó Ceallaigh | 1987- |

# GLOSSARY

*black friars:* those Franciscans who did not conform to the reform in Ireland at the end of the nineteenth century.

*brown friars:* the Franciscans who adopted the reform in Ireland at the end of the nineteenth century.

*chapter:* a meeting of representatives of the friars for the purpose of electing superiors and passing legislation; a general chapter involves the friars of the whole world, a provincial chapter those of a particular province.

*chapter bill:* a document produced after a provincial chapter which lists new appointments and may indicate changes in legislation.

*conferences, theological:* regular meetings of priests at which items of a theological nature are discussed with the aim of keeping the clergy abreast of the teaching of the Church on theological matters.

*congregation:* the title given to a provincial chapter at which major superiors (the provincial and his definitorium) are not elected.

*constitutions, general:* a basic code of law giving the spiritual principles covering the entire Order.

*convent:* technically a 'formed house' with a community of at least six religious (according to old Church law) living in a house which has been legally erected; used in a wide sense to mean the part of a friary building where the friars actually live (see 'residence').

*Conventual:* term applied to the non-reform group within the Order in the sixteenth century, and the name applied to that group after the Order was split into two Orders in 1517; this Order died out in Ireland after the Reformation.

*custody:* an administrative unit within a province of the Order, governed by a custos; under certain circumstances, it may be independent.

*definitor:* member of the inner council which advises and guides the minister general or the minister provincial on the running of the Order or the province.

*erect:* legal term covering the formalities of settling up a house in law by obtaining the necessary permissions from the local bishop.

*faculties:* the permission given by a bishop or a major superior to priests so that they may administer the sacraments (in particular penance) and preach.

*foundation:* a term governing the permission given in writing by the local bishop by which a convent may be erected in law, and includes permission for a public church; sometimes incorrectly used about permission for a residence.

158 *friary:* generally used in English to mean any place where friars live,

be it a convent or a residence.

*general:* the head of the Franciscan Order; the full title is minister general; the vicar general governs the Order in the absence of the minister general, but this has also been used as a title for a person governing large sections of the Order and responsible only to the minister general; the procurator general is the chief adviser to the minister general and handles relations with the Roman Curia; a commissary general and a delegate general are people to whom the minister general has delegated part of his authority to deal with particular problems or special circumstances; for visitator general, see 'visitator'.

*guardian:* the superior of a convent, thus giving rise to the term guardianate for such a house; in Ireland a tradition arose by which friars were nominated titular guardians to old convents where there were no longer resident communities.

*mission:* an organized group of friars living in a foreign country and trying to instil the faith there; or a period of special preaching within a Christianized country, with the aim of deepening the faith.

*Observant:* term applied to the reform group within the Order in the fifteenth century, and the names applied to that group after the Order was split into two Orders in 1517; the use of the term ceased towards 1700; the reform movement is found in other Orders but I have used it in a specific Franciscan sense.

*province:* the Franciscan Order is divided, for administrative purposes, into provinces, each of which is quasi-autonomous; the friar who governs the province is the minister provincial and his assistant is the vicar provincial; this latter title is also used for the friar who rules the province in the absence of the minister provincial, or who governs part of the province in his own right; the term 'vice-province' has been introduced for an administrative unit created by gathering various friaries together, which is governed by a provincial and will soon become a province.

*president:* the superior of a residence.

*quest:* the seeking of alms from lay people by the friars.

*regulars:* religious who take solemn vows and thus belong to an Order, as distinct from those who take simple vows and belong to a congregation; in practice, those who belong to the monastic Orders (monks) or mendicant Orders (friars) and who are exempt from the authority of the local bishop.

*residence:* any house where religious live and which has not been erected into a foundation, either because there is not a sufficient number of religious in the community, or because the local bishop will not permit a full foundation; term no longer in use since all   159 friars have to be assigned to a guardianate even if living alone.

*Restoration:* the period immediately following the restoration of Charles II to the English throne in 1660.

*Seraphic:* the title Seraphic is proper to the Franciscans, just as the title Angelic is proper to the Dominicans; a seraphic college is a minor seminary for training candidates to the Order.

*statutes:* while constitutions detail the spiritual principles proper to the whole Order, laws proper to particular sections of the Order, either administrative or territorial, are called statutes.

*Suppression:* the period during which the buildings belonging to the various Orders in Ireland were confiscated by the civil authority and the communities dispersed; in practice, 1536 to *c.* 1550.

*visitator:* at regular intervals of three or six years a representative of the general or the provincial himself pays an official visit to all the houses within a province, correcting faults or consulting the friars on various matters: recent usage prefers the word 'visitor'.

# BIBLIOGRAPHY

Bradshaw, B., *The Dissolution of the Religious Orders in Ireland under Henry VIII* (Cambridge 1974).

Brady, J., 'Some Aspects of the Irish Church in the Eighteenth Century' in *IER*, LXX (1948), 515-23.

—, *Catholics and Catholicism in the Eighteenth Century Press* (Maynooth 1965).

Buckley, J. J., 'Some Irish Altar Plate' in *JRSAI* (supplementary vol.) (1943).

Burke, W. P., *The Irish Priests in Penal Times* (Waterford 1914).

Byrne, C. J., *Gentlemen-Bishops and Faction Fighters* (St John's, Newfoundland 1948).

Clyn, J., ofm, *The Annals of Ireland by Friar John Clyn and Thady Dowling*, (ed.) R. Butler (Dublin 1849).

Colledge, E. (ed.), *The Latin Poems of Richard Ledred, ofm, Bishop of Ossory, 1317-60* (Toronto 1974).

Concannon, T., *The Poor Clares in Ireland* (Dublin 1929).

Conlan, P., ofm, 'A Short Title Calendar of Material Relating to Ireland in the General Archives of the Franciscan Order in Rome', *Coll. Hib.*, 18-28 (1976-86).

—, *St Isidore's Rome* (Rome 1982).

—, 'The Irish Franciscans in Newfoundland' in *The Past*, 15, (1984), 69-76.

—, 'The Irish Franciscans in Australia in the Nineteenth Century' in *Footprints* (Melbourne), IV-VI (1981-7).

—, 'The Irish Franciscans in China' in *The Brief* (1986-7).

—, 'The Outlaw Friary of Athlone' in *Jn. Old Ath. Soc.*, 5 (1978), 38-44.

—, *A True Franciscan . . . Br Paschal* (Gormanston 1978)

—, 'Vocations to the Irish Franciscans, 1800-1980' in *Arch. Hib.* XLIV (1988), 29-37.

Egan, B., ofm, 'An Annotated Calendar of the O'Meara Papers' in *Arch. Fran. Hist.* 68 (1975), 78-110 & 366-408.

Faulkner, A., ofm (ed.), *Liber Dubliniensis, Chapter Documents of the Irish Franciscans, 1719-1875* (Killiney 1978).

Fenning, H., op, *The Undoing of the Friars of Ireland: a study of the novitiate question in the eighteenth century* (Louvain 1972).

Fitzmaurice, E. B., ofm, & Little, A. G., *Materials for the History of the Franciscan Province in Ireland A.D. 1230-1450* (Manchester 1920).

Giblin, C., ofm, 'Aspects of Franciscan Life in Ireland in the Seventeenth Century' in *Fran. Coll. Ann.* (Multyfarnham) (1948), 67-72.

—, 'Daniel O'Connell and the Irish Franciscans' in *Fran. Coll. Ann.* (Multyfarnham) (1950), 69-78 & 80.

—, 'A Seventeenth Century Idea: Two Franciscan Provinces in Ireland' in *Fran. Coll. Ann.* (Multyfarnham) (1951), 55-67.

—, *Liber Lovaniensis: a collection of Irish Franciscan documents, 1629-1717* (Dublin 1956).

—, *The Irish Franciscan Mission to Scotland, 1619-46* (Dublin 1964).

Gwynn, A. & Hadcock, R. N., *Medieval Religious Houses Ireland* (London 1971).

Hoade, E. & Mooney, C., ofm, 'Ireland and the Holy Land' in *Fran. Coll. Ann.* (Multyfarnham) (1952), 69-77.

Hunt, J., *Irish Medieval Figure Sculpture* (2 vols, Dublin 1974).

Leask, H. G., *Irish Churches and Monastic Buildings* (3 vols, Dundalk 1955-66).

McGrath, K., 'John Garzia, a noted priest catcher, and his activities 1717-23' in *IER*, LXXI (1949), 494-514.

—, 'The Irish Franciscans in the Eighteenth Century' in *Fran. Coll. Ann.* (Multyfarnham) (1950), 53-8.

—, 'Sidelights on the Irish Franciscans, 1798-1850', in *Fran. Coll. Ann.* (Multyfarnham) (1952), 81-8.

Mac Guaire, S., cssr., 'Ireland and the Catholic Hebrides' in *IER*, XLII, (1933), 488-99.

Matthews, [*alias* O'Mahoney] F., ofm, 'Brevis synopsis provinciae Hiberniae fratrum minorum', (ed.) B. Jennings ofm, *Anal. Hib.*, 6 (1934), 139-91.

Millet, B., ofm, *The Irish Franciscans 1651-65* (Rome 1964).

Mooney, C., ofm, 'The Golden Age of the Irish Franciscans' in S. O'Brien ofm (ed.), *Measgra i gCuimhne Mhichíl Uí Chléirigh* (Dublin 1944), 21-33.

—, *Devotional Writings of the Irish Franciscans, 1224-1950* (Killiney 1952).

—, 'The Franciscans in Ireland' in *Terminus*, VIII-XIV (1954-7).

—, 'Franciscan Architecture in Pre-Reformation Ireland' in *JRSAI*, LXXXV-LXXXVII (1955-7).

—, 'The Irish Franciscans 1650-99 in *Catholic Survey* (Galway 1953), 378-402.

—, *Scríbhinní Foireann Taighde Dhún Mhuire, 1945-70* (Killiney 1971).

—, 'De provincia Hiberniae S. Francisci' (ed.) B. Jennings, ofm, *Anal. Hib.*, 6 (1934), 12-38.

Murphy, D., sj, *Our Martyrs* (Dublin 1896).

Shaw, N., ofm cap., *The Irish Capuchins . . . 1885-1985* (Dublin 1985).

—, *Sisters of St Clare* (Dublin 1985).

Walsh, K., *A Fourteenth-Century Scholar and Primate: Richard FitzRalph in Oxford, Avignon and Armagh* (Oxford 1981).

Watt, J. A., *The Church and the Two Nations in Medieval Ireland* (Cambridge 1970).

—, *The Church in Medieval Ireland* (Dublin 1972).

# ABBREVIATIONS

Anal Hib.
 Analecta Hibernica
Arch. Fran. Hib.
 Archivum Franciscanum
 Historicum
Arch. Hib.
 Archivium Hibernicum
Coll. Hib.
 Collectanea Hibernica
Clogh. Rec.
 Clogher Record
Don. Ann.
 Donegal Annual
Fran. Coll. Ann.
 Franciscan College Annual
IER
 Irish Ecclesiastical Record
JACAS
 Journal of the Ardagh and
 Clonmacnois Antiquarian
 Society
JCHAS
 Journal of the Cork Historical
 and Archaeological Society

JGAHS
 Journal of the Galway Archaeo-
 logical and Historical Society
JKAHS
 Journal of the Kerry Archaeo-
 logical and Historical Society
JKAS
 Journal of the Kildare Archaeo-
 logical Society
JOAS
 Journal of the Old Athlone
 Society
JRSAI
 Journal of the Royal Society
 of Antiquaries of Ireland
OKR
 Old Kilkenny Review
NMAJ
 North Munster Antiquarian
 Journal
SEAN. ARDMH.
 Seanchas Ardmhacha
UJA
 Ulster Journal of Archaeology

# INDEX

Numbers in **bold** refer to references in Gazetteer.